THE PURSUIT OF QUALITY
THROUGH PERSONAL CHANGE

THE PURSUIT OF QUALITY THROUGH PERSONAL CHANGE

Harry I. Forsha

ASQC Quality Press
Milwaukee, Wisconsin

THE PURSUIT OF QUALITY THROUGH PERSONAL CHANGE
Harry I. Forsha

Library of Congress Cataloging-in-Publication Data
Forsha, Harry I.
   The pursuit of quality through personal change / Harry I. Forsha.
      p.   cm.
   Includes bibliographical references and index.
   ISBN 0–87389–140–6
   1. Customer relations. 2. Customer service.
   3. Quality of products   I. Title.
   HF5415.5.F67   1991
   658.8'12—dc20   91–34376
                                                              CIP

10 9 8 7 6 5 4 3 2 1

ISBN 0–87389–140–6

Acquisitions Editor: Jeanine L. Lau
Production Editor: Mary Beth Nilles
Set in Sabon by A-R Editions, Inc.
Cover and interior design by A-R Editions, Inc.
Printed and bound by BookCrafters

For a free copy of the ASQC Quality Press Publications Catalog,
including ASQC membership information, call 800-952-6587.

Printed in the United States of America

 Printed on recycled paper

ASQC Quality Press
611 East Wisconsin Avenue
Milwaukee, Wisconsin 53202

To my wife, Diane;
my children, Elizabeth and Christopher;
and my friend, Dave

Contents

Foreword

During May of 1990, I had a chance to meet Harry Forsha at one of our KAIZEN seminars in the United States. During the course of several interchanges about his book and KAIZEN I found his ideas interesting and supportive of the continual improvement process.

Continual improvement, or in Japanese, KAIZEN, has been used by companies all over the world increasingly during the last ten years. The practice has followed a trend in every company that has initiated it. Usually there is an emphasis on increased inspection and then a switch to control of process using statistics. Later on attention is placed on upstream management in areas such as corporate planning and design.

As Harry points out in this book, the process usually arrives at its critical point when individuals, regardless of where they are positioned, find out that it is very personal. They—we—have to deal with the basic issues of our own goals, motivation and behaviors. We have to ask the "hard 5 why questions" to determine ability to stick with it.

The hardest part of continual improvement is **creating the will to make it happen.** If we do not search our personal rationale and align it with the direction that our organizations are going we will have problems.

Once on a personal path for improvement, we can tie-in techniques without the additional complication of managing relationships, and with good chances for success. A healthy understanding of our own process of change can help us begin to work with others.

As you read this book and either begin or continue with your own personal or corporate process of continual improvement, I challenge you, the reader, not to just "study it," but to "do it"!

Masaaki Imai

Preface

In his book *Critical Path*, R. Buckminster Fuller described a major change in his career and his life:

> In 1927, at the age of 32, finding myself a "throwaway" in the business world, I sought to . . . discover what if anything a healthy young male human of average size, experience, and capability with an economically dependent wife and newborn child, starting without capital or any kind of wealth, cash savings, account monies, credit, or university degree, could effectively do that could not be done by great nations or great private enterprise. . .

It can be comforting to know that great thinkers have many of the same everyday problems and challenges that we all face. Yet, if we could capture their solutions to these problems or their process for dealing with challenges, perhaps we could each improve our own well-being.

If we can stop asking, "What can I do?" and ask instead, "What *can* I do?", then we have taken the first step. There is always something we can do. We just need to identify it and make a commitment to do it.

Those who are totally satisfied with everything in their lives and careers need not read this book. For the rest of us, the following pages contain simple, practical concepts and methods to improve the quality of our lives and businesses, beginning with the process of personal change. If we can apply these methods and concepts, perhaps we can each capture a little more of the greatness we all have within us.

Acknowledgments

I would like to express my deep appreciation to those who have been helpful to me in preparing this book: to Dave Rogers, of the Center for Individual Growth, for his insights into organizational behavior, his encouragement, and especially his friendship; to my friends Belen Marrero and John Batcheller, of Florida Power and Light, and to John Tucker, now with Tampa Armature Works, who first introduced me to quality improvement concepts, and to Florida Power and Light for graciously allowing me to make use of their materials; to Jim Killingsworth of QUALTEC, who provided valuable insight and assistance, particularly on quality management issues; to Stuart Chalmers and Kim Kaddatz, of the KAIZEN® Institute, who shared their wealth of personal experience and background in practical implementation, to John Lowman, who is largely responsible for the statistical tools section, and most of all to Masaaki Imai; to Judith Schalick of the Juran Institute, for her powerful insight into senior management behaviors; to Arnold Harrington, Jake Turner, and Bubba Turner, and my friends and associates at Tampa Armature Works, for creating a work environment which encouraged creative thinking and continuous improvement; and most of all, to my editor, Jeanine Lau, of ASQC Quality Press, without whose encouragement this book would not have been possible.

Section One

PERSONAL CHANGE

One

INTRODUCTION

The objective of this book is to provide a clearly written, easy-to-understand guide to the process of quality improvement through personal change. It is inspired by the writings of R. Buckminster Fuller, Philip B. Crosby, W. Edwards Deming, J. M. Juran, and Masaaki Imai. The comments and ideas of many friends and associates are also used as examples of the wide varieties of creative thinking and resources available if you know where to look and how to listen.

The purpose here is to fill a gap. There are many books written on the subject of quality improvement. Even though they profess to be simple, most are aimed at the serious student who has a strong academic background. It also helps if the reader of these books is in a position to directly influence the policies of her or his company. This book is about creating meaningful personal change, regardless of one's position in a company or whether the company has a quality improvement program. This same personal process can then be expanded to deal with associates, groups, and organizations.

This book is *not* about statistical process control (SPC), otherwise known as quality control. Quality control is based on the concept of reducing variation in situations where consistency has a positive value. This book deals with the concept of continuous improvement. It is based on the idea that change is fundamental to both life and work, and that these changes cannot always be controlled. When change can and should be controlled, SPC is appropriate. When changes are outside our span of control, such as the number of incoming jobs in a service business, statistics may be used to observe and quantify change, rather than control it.

Some people are destined to change the world. For most of us, however, it is all we can do to manage our own affairs. Regardless of whether you select a personal or worldwide range, you must begin with personal change. Why?

Because changes result from actions. If *you* want to change something, then the action must come from *you*. To do otherwise is to remove yourself from the process. To remove yourself from the process may very well eliminate any hope you have of influencing the results.

The creation of personal change is a process. It is the most important process because it feeds all other activities. With understanding and mastery of this process, you can accomplish a great deal. Many people cited in this book have accomplished great things, yet each of them had obstacles to overcome along the way. Failures in quality improvement can occur because the process of change (not the problem-solving process) is poorly understood and executed. This obstacle can be overcome by defining the process of change, exploring each step along the way, and learning, through practice, how to manage the process step-by-step.

Everyone likes the idea of quality. But until we agree on a definition of quality, we can't even begin to work toward it. Let's begin with a basic definition, as stated by my friend, Benny Darsey, of Tampa Armature Works: "Quality is conformance to requirements. Everything else is bull. . . ."

This is not the only definition of quality, but it is a convenient place to start. The word "quality" is often confused with the word "premium." Benny summarized the thinking of many quality professionals: People want what they want when they want it. They don't want something else, they don't want less than they want, and they certainly don't want it at some other time. And, while we're at it, folks usually have a value in mind which is translated into a "fair price" for their need. Identifying this perceived value and meeting it is another part of quality (or in other words, another requirement). Specific, tried-and-true problem-solving "tools" help to identify and conform to established requirements. These same tools can help define additional requirements that may be needed. Many of these tools may seem cold or cut-and-dried. They will only become warm when they have a direct use to you in accomplishing your goals. Each tool will be described in turn in a basic, concrete way which will allow its immediate use.

Having accomplished change in yourself, you may want to broaden your influence. This will require a further knowledge of your role in groups, types of group behavior, and the ways to use the quality tools you have already learned . . . this time fine-tuned for use in a group setting.

The fourth section of this book deals with changing management attitudes. This subject is approached from the standpoint that managers are people, too. If we can understand what kind of people they are, and where they are in the process of change, we can better work together with them to take the best action for ourselves and our organizations.

Finally, references to books, audiotapes, and videotapes are provided to help expand your in-depth knowledge in each area covered.

It is my hope that this material is simple, personal, practical, and enjoyable. If you can create change in yourself (and make it stick), then you can influence your environment, your community, and your workplace.

Maybe even the world.

Good luck.

Two

THE PROCESS OF
PERSONAL CHANGE

Quality is simple; people are complicated. Achieving quality in life or at work can be treated as a process of methodically simplifying our thinking to root out the distractions and focus on the important issues. Many well-known quality improvement regimens take an extra step to help define the important issues. Juran, for example, deals with the importance of planning; Crosby is well-known for the concept of zero defects and cost of quality; Deming has his famous 14 points. These issues can be handled in an organization by use of functional deployment, that is, applying the skills of many individuals to a problem. On a personal level, individual initiative and personal strengths can be applied to the improvement process. In this chapter, important personal and organizational concepts are combined to provide a total approach to continuous improvement. Examples will be used to show how these concepts can be used in both individual and organizational situations.

By combining ideas from the areas of personal improvement, organizational behavior, and structured problem solving, we can develop a simple and powerful methodology. This methodology is based on five assertions:

1. Conformance to requirements (one definition of quality) can be used as a basis for improvement activities.

2. The process of personal change can be defined, described, and managed.

3. The same process of personal change can be applied to groups in a structured way to produce group improvements.

4. Structured problem-solving techniques can be applied to both personal and business situations.

5. Change is ever present, so individual and group processes are always in motion.

In other words, we can start from the process of individual change, and build outward to relationships, groups, and organizations, applying relationship tools and quality tools in a structured way to produce desired changes.

The process of personal change can be expressed simply: Develop a vision, establish commitment, then make it happen. Although this is a good description of what needs to be done, it is very general.

Figure 2.1 outlines the process of personal change as we will discuss it. The diagram shows two possible paths in the process. The way the process is handled is the key to continuous improvement. If the desired result is simply adjustment to change, then the path marked "adjustment" can be taken. If the desired result is to influence the direction of change or to create change, then the "action" path must be taken. The process of personal change is the first step on the path to continuous improvement.

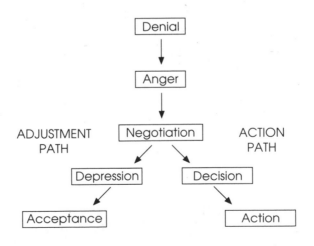

FIGURE 2.1. The process of personal change[1]

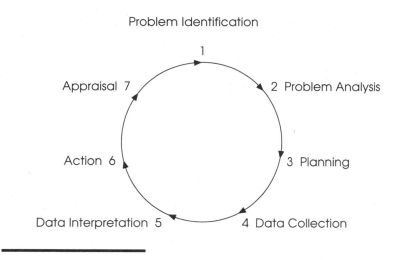

FIGURE 2.2 The quality improvement process[2]

Once the "action" path has been completed, the quality improvement process can be applied. The seven-step quality improvement process is the second step in the path to continuous improvement. This process consists of seven parts (see Figure 2.2). By applying the quality improvement process to the act of personal change, we create a powerful technique for everyday use.

An improved understanding of the process of personal change coupled with the consistent application of quality tools can lead to continuous improvement.

In the process of change, as in any other process, each step must be taken in turn. To attempt step two before completing step one is like trying to wax your car before you have washed it. The result will not be pretty. To apply this process to the wrong issue is like waxing your pet cockateil.

Once the process is understood, problems (or opportunities, if you prefer) can be diagnosed by identifying the stage of the process where they occurred, then rethinking the effort made at that stage. Once you are familiar with the continuous improvement process, you will be able to trace a problem stepwise back through your personal actions until you have found the stage deserving attention. Having observed this critical point in the process, you can make your correction and forge ahead.

Let's look a little closer at the process of personal change.

IDENTIFYING THE NEED FOR CHANGE

If quality can be defined as conformance to requirements, then what are *your* requirements? Why do *you* want to change? This seems like a simple question. In order to make a good judgment regarding the need (or lack of need) for personal change, you must be in touch with yourself. Getting in touch with yourself is a process, too. There are many paths to personal awareness. Some people choose spiritual methods, some use a psychological approach, some use rational thinking. Regardless of the path you select, you must still get through each of the five stages of personal change.

Fritz Perls uses the analogy that self-discovery is like peeling an onion, one layer at a time.[3] With each layer can come pleasant surprises and deep satisfaction. Sometimes you may also uncover hidden difficulties, but most of them can be overcome. With each layer your goals may change, sometimes dramatically.

How do you know when you are finished? The best explanation I have heard comes from the Dale Carnegie radio commercial you may have heard. It is the story of an old man who is polishing an intricately carved brass door. A passerby commented on the care with which the old man approached his work, and asked when he would be finished. The old man replied, "Oh, I'm never finished. I just keep polishing until they take it away."

Like the old man with the door, we are never finished with self-discovery. We only get closer and closer. As you get deeper, you will find that your goal is more constant, the adjustments are smaller, and you will be more comfortable with change. If this happens as you work your plan, then you are headed in the right direction. It is the process of continual improvement, or in Japanese, *kaizen,* that forms the basis of this book. By first understanding what it is we want to change, by "defining our requirements," we can gradually change our activities to accomplish our objectives. We can frequently accomplish a great deal more by constant, gradual improvement than by trying to make a major change all at once.

The "Five Whys," popularized by Ohno, make a good test to determine if you're ready for change.[4] You can use the question "why?" to peel your "personal onion." Imagine someone asking you why you want to change. If you don't have an immediate answer that is rock-solid to you, then you're not ready. If your plan doesn't hang together or if daily events make you want to change course, you're not ready. If, on the other hand, you can give an instant, solid, common-sense answer to the question "why do you want to do that?", then you are applying the process of change to the right issue.

If you are really adventurous, ask the question, "why?", in response to each previous answer. Do this five times. If you get past three, you're doing well.

Here's an example: Your friend, Fred, says he wants to quit his job. You ask, "Why?" "Because I am dissatisfied with my job." "Why?" "Because I'm not making enough money." At this point, it gets interesting. Is Fred not making enough money because his boss is a cheapskate? Is it because Fred does not have the negotiating skills necessary to get the best deal for himself? Is it because Fred isn't doing a good job by his boss' standards, but the boss never told him? Is it because his boss gave him objectives, but Fred did not possess the listening skills to hear them? As you can see, the first few "whys" get you past the superficial level to the meat of the issue. Now, let's go one step further. Assume that the problem is Fred's negotiating skills.

"Fred, why do you not have the negotiating skills?" "Because I never got the training." "Why didn't you do whatever was necessary to get the training you needed?" We have now arrived at a critical point, and it's very personal. In order to answer the last question, Fred will have to deal with the basic issues of his own personal goals, his motivation, and his behaviors. As we get to the third why and beyond, the questions should be asked by ourselves, not by others.

It is not hard to see why the process of asking "why?" five times will help us peel our onion. The process of digging for deeper, more basic solutions is a powerful part of continuous improvement. By making the Five Whys a part of ourselves, we have a tool for identifying basic, fundamental, comprehensive changes in our attitudes and behaviors that can have wide-ranging benefits. The result of this effort can be improvements that will affect not only the problem at hand (in our example, the job) but perhaps many other issues at the same time (in our example, personal goals and motivation).

But we have gotten a little ahead of ourselves. Let's back up to the beginning of the process of change. As stated earlier, there are five steps, as shown in Figure 2.1. The first three are always the same. The last two depend on the path taken in step three.

THE PROCESS OF CHANGE

The diagram in Figure 2.1 can be applied to both individual and group situations. For now, we will focus on the way this process works on a personal level. As has been emphasized, the process must proceed step-by-step. If we can observe where we are, we can then determine what actions may be appropriate at the time.

Denial

We enter into the process of change when we become aware that a need for change exists. So long as there is no awareness, we will have no need to change. There is no opportunity to deny something we don't know about. Yet we often select our awareness by area of interest. For instance, some people are environmentalists, some are intellectuals, some are extremely religious. All these words express areas or types of interests. Someone interested in a particular subject is more likely to be aware of items relating to their area of interest.

Denial, on the other hand, occurs where we are aware of information, and choose to ignore (or deny) the information. This is not the same as choosing not to take action on known information. This is denying the information that has been presented to us. Management by fact is a tool which helps us eliminate denial.

We all have certain opinions about the way things are. Yet experience has taught me that any actual situation is usually somewhat different (if not vastly different) than my original opinion. By taking the trouble to identify and quantify the facts relating to each issue, we ensure that we are headed in the right direction.

Actual numerical data are facts which are hard to refute and make a powerful weapon in the war against denial. Later on, this tool can also be used for interpersonal communication, particularly if the numbers are presented in graphic form. We may even need to establish a measuring system to determine just what the facts are.

Once we have examined the numerical and other facts about a situation, we are in a position to determine if it is truly worthy of additional attention. If it is, we move on to the next step.

Anger

Anger is a secondary emotion. In other words, it is a reaction to some other emotional condition, like fear or insecurity. Regardless of its source, anger is the second stage of change. We may not always experience anger. If we did a good job of examining the facts (avoiding denial), we will not be surprised that some problem is worthy of our attention. We may still experience anger with ourselves if the facts point to our own "stupid mistakes." That's OK, as long as we get over it.

Anger frequently occurs as a result of surprise. The "shoot the messenger" syndrome is a good example. For example, you discover that the telephone system is disconnecting customers when it should be transferring calls. Proud of your discovery and ready to take corrective action, you bring this information to your boss. He explodes, insulting the phone system, the supplier of the system, and you, too. The explosion may not be an expression of an actual problem with you. Yet, the result of such an uprising is that the messenger is unlikely to carry any other negative information (important or otherwise) to the boss. This situation can be extremely dangerous since much useful information is negative in nature (for instance, the building is on fire). In order to proceed on a constructive course, we must get past the anger and settle back down to producing change (putting the fire out).

Negotiation

This step contains a critical point. Jongaeward suggests that there are six ways of reacting to new information.[5] Your choice at this point will determine if you are going to produce change or adapt to a change that has been imposed on you. In other words, change or be changed. Here are the six options:

1. Withdrawal
2. Rituals
3. Pastimes
4. Activities
5. Games
6. Authentic confrontation

The first five options describe ways of filling our time so that we do not have to engage in authentic confrontation. What makes this particularly personal is that the authentic confrontation must be with oneself. If we choose options one to five, we will travel along the left-hand side of the wishbone diagram in Figure 2.1, toward depression and acceptance. If we choose authentic confrontation, we proceed down the right side, toward decision and action.

Depression and Acceptance

This path is not all bad. There are some situations that are beyond our control. Nevertheless, we must pass through these stages or the issue will remain an emotional open item until we do. If we can understand that we are hung up in the depression stage, we can consider what it will take to get us out of it. Once we have reached the acceptance stage, we are ready to go on to something else.

Decision and Action

This path applies to areas where we wish to take an active part in producing change. We must bring ourselves to the point of deciding to take some action, and then committing to do it. Once we have reached the action stage, we can apply structured problem solving to determine exactly what action to take and with what expected results.

Summary

The five-step process is not the only way to look at change. But it provides a useful framework for examining the process of change, observing our personal behavior, determining where in the process we are, diagnosing problem areas, and pointing the direction for future activities.

CONSIDERING THE OPTIONS

You probably have many more than one personal requirement—no doubt you have several items on your list. Let's focus for a moment on the things you would like to change. The starting point is defining your requirements. What do *you* want? When you can answer this question, you have a solid starting point for developing what Juran calls the "breakthrough attitude" necessary to mobilize for change.

Your requirements can be defined only by you, and they can change from time to time. The process of change must be relevant to you if you are to succeed in accomplishing your goals, and if you want to feel good about yourself along the way. The following sections deal with a method for narrowing the field of issues down to the "vital few" issues of greatest importance. We can begin with the use of brainstorming, the structured technique for generating ideas. Table 2.1 lists the rules for brainstorming.

Do take time out to brainstorm in a relaxing environment.

Do think about what you want to change. What makes you angry or causes personal stress?

Each time you think of a new idea, write it down.

Do not exclude anything or rule anything out.

Do not analyze, question, or challenge any idea.

TABLE 2.1 Rules for brainstorming

Keep your list with you for a while—a day or a week—until you're sure you have listed all the important things you want to change. Ideas will sneak up on you at the strangest times. Be prepared. Many great ideas have been lost to history for the lack of a pencil.

Remember that at this point you are only generating ideas. If you don't have a page full of things you could improve, you're not trying hard enough.

Establishing Priorities

Why go to all this trouble? It goes back to the need that you are about to encounter: developing commitment. It's hard to become committed to an unimportant task, something else will always get in the way. If you are unsure about your goals or objectives, it is likely that halfway through this process something else will come up which is more important and you'll be off in another direction. As a result, you will have expended time and energy without having accomplishing anything. Although it is sometimes necessary to change directions, in many cases it can be unnecessary aggravation.

It is important to establish clear priorities. But once we have done that, many of us can work on more than one task at a time.

Or can we?

To be honest with ourselves, we cannot do the best job on one item if we are distracted by another. *So why try?* Do one thing at a time. I heard the story of a man who was eating a doughnut, drinking coffee, and talking on a cellular phone while driving a car. End result: He ran into a telephone pole. Get the message?

Much has been written about managing multiple priorities, but doesn't it all boil down to taking care of the number one item first? There is a reason, in our example, why driving the car should be the number one priority. The same is true of other situations. If by asking "why?", we can understand the reasons for our actions, we can make sure that we do the right thing first.

Narrow the list generated by brainstorming down to your top few items, or as Juran calls it, the "vital few." Take a sheet of lined paper and divide it into three columns. Spread your items along the left column from top to bottom. This will get you ready for the next step. By this time, you should have no doubt that the items you are now considering are the most important to you. Figure 2.3 shows a sample list.

Goal Selection and Setting

The objective of this section is to help you prioritize your list. "These are the things I would like to change." Your ideas are already listed on the left third of a piece of lined paper. You have

PROPOSED CHANGE

Get in shape

Learn to play the piano

Start a savings plan

Feel useful to others

Be free of habits

FIGURE 2.3 Short list of issues

reduced your list to no more than seven items. If you have second thoughts, then match the new ideas against the ones already on the page. If a new idea is more important than one already on the page, make the substitution. When you are finished, you will have the top seven items (or less). These should be absolutely the most important issues to you.

Next, make a second column (you will make three columns in all). In the second column put the expected result of the change. Be as specific as possible. Imagine what it will be like when you have accomplished this goal. Describe it in words. Imagination can be a powerful force, so take the time to create a clear mental image. Do this for each item. Figure 2.4 shows how this was done for our example.

Finally in the third column, we must define an indicator of progress. The definition of indicate is to point out, signify, denote, show, manifest, mark, disclose, or reveal.

In order to have an indicator that does one of the things listed in our definition, you must have something that is real, observable, and measurable. See Figure 2.5 for a few examples. You may know of several indicators for one goal. List them all. Later, you will select the indicator which will work best for you.

You may find that some of your ideas are difficult to quantify. Don't let this stand in your way. As in all barriers, you must overcome it. Work as hard as you must to get this list completed. If an item is not important enough to spend the time on, then remove it from the list.

PROPOSED CHANGE	EXPECTED RESULT
Get in shape	I walk down the beach. Women (men) are amazed at the balance and perfection of my beautiful body.
Learn to play the piano	We are sitting in a living room. Several friends are gathered around a grand piano, singing along while I play.
Start a savings plan	It is the sixth of the month. I get my bank statement and more money is coming in than going out. I feel so good, I buy myself an ice cream cone.
Feel useful to others	It is Thanksgiving and I am cooking soup at the church kitchen, so that we can feed the homeless people.
Be free of habits	I walk past the vending machine with a smile on my face and change in my pocket.

FIGURE 2.4 Short list with expected results

There are two schools of thought about feasibility. Some people think you should consider only those items that are within your control. Certainly, there is merit to this approach. On the other hand, should we not also consider those things that are important, but beyond our control? I like the second approach. If an issue is beyond your control, look at it realistically and determine what is needed to overcome the obstacles. Don't give up on an issue just because it's tough. Sometimes surmounting the tough problems gives us the greatest sense of satisfaction.

So far, you have accomplished the following:

1. Defined your personal requirements.
2. Listed items you would like to change.
3. Reduced the list to the most important items.

PROPOSED CHANGE	EXPECTED RESULT	INDICATOR
Get in shape	Beach . . . body.	Weight, waist measurement, muscle tone
Learn to play the piano	Living room . . . singing along.	List of songs, invitations to play
Start a savings plan	Money in bank . . . ice cream cone.	Account balance
Feel useful to others	Thanksgiving . . . church kitchen.	Days of service, Contributions
Be free of habits	Vending machine . . . change.	No stops

FIGURE 2.5 Short list with expected results and indicators

4. Described the intended results.
5. Established indicators of success by which to measure the results.

Now, it's time to work this list.

Challenging Your Thinking

As we said earlier, the concept of quality is simple. It is people who are complex. After you have completed your list, you will probably still be turning these ideas over in your subconscious mind. You will find that other ideas may pop up in the next few days. Write them down. When you are sure that your list is final, it is time to challenge your thinking. You will now switch from philosopher to analyst. Look at each item in turn.

Proposed Change

Is this actually something you want to change? "Maybe" means you have done some fuzzy thinking. Choose either yes or no, or go back to the drawing board. If the answer is "no," strike the item from your list.

Expected Result

You should have a clear mental picture of what you want the result to be. Again, if the vision is fuzzy, go back to the drawing board until you can create a clear picture.

Indicator

You absolutely must know how you will measure your progress. There are many reasons for this, but among the most important is that we tend to feel lost or useless when we're not making progress. Unless you can *see* the progress, you may become discouraged. Unless you can measure your results, you will never be able to see your progress.

The importance of the psychological effect of measurement is wonderfully summarized by Crosby's saying, "what gets measured gets done."[6]

Now that you have reviewed your proposed changes, expected results, and indicators, and have corrected any fuzzy thinking and dropped items from the list that are not deserving of your attention, you're ready to begin the seven-step process of structured problem solving.

It may seem like the long way to get started, but it has been my experience that focusing on activities is the first key in producing results.

First Things First

Crosby is well known for the phrase, "do it right the first time."[7] The hard part is deciding what "it" is.

Look at your prioritized list. Look at the first item and challenge yourself. Is there any reason at all why this should not be the first item? If the first item should be replaced by the second, do that now. Review each item in turn until you are absolutely certain which is the most important. By now, you have:

1. Decided which item is absolutely the most important thing to do.
2. Clearly identified your objective.
3. Established a measurable indicator so that you can see your progress.

You have now reduced your list to the number one item and are almost ready to go on to the next step of the process, problem analysis. (Why only one item at a time? Remember the guy who ran into the telephone pole?)

There is one major point remaining before we can proceed: establishing commitment. If there is one single item in this process that will save you time and effort, it is taking the time to establish commitment before you go to the trouble of attempting change. Let's take a moment now to finish cementing the proposed change by establishing commitment.

Establishing Commitment

Let's review our progress up to this point. You have now selected your goal. You do not have the problem of something more important coming up because you have thoroughly reviewed your situation, listed your options, and selected the best one on which to start.

There are three key words that are all-important to progress:

1. Motivation
2. Commitment
3. Self-discipline

Each, in its own way, can make the difference between success and failure. Let's examine them, one at a time. Motivation: that which leads to *action*. Each of us is motivated by different things. Reduced to the simplest form, our motivation is either to approach something or to get away from it. What leads *you* to action?

EXAMPLES

Approach	Avoidance
Acquisition	Fear of failure
Friendship	Fear of success
Curiosity	Fear of confrontation
Challenge	Fear of the unknown

Many books and tapes deal exclusively with motivation. The brief list above is intended only to raise the issue. Each of us must deal with it individually. You should know your motivation for your number one item, as a result of all the work you have already done. Remember the Five Whys and test yourself again. Are you prepared, on a basic emotional level, to undertake the most difficult job you have ever had? If you are not ready, what will it take to get you ready? The daily newspapers provide many examples of situations that were known to be problems, but had to get sufficiently horrible before corrective action was taken. That's usually the high-cost solution in terms of time, energy, and money. It's much easier, although it takes more discipline, to plan ahead. If you don't need to change anything now, don't change. And yet the habit of continuous improvement, if practiced daily, can be a valuable discipline when a large problem comes along.

In order to build this discipline of continuous improvement, we've got to be excited about change, because most people have a vested interest in keeping things the same. For example, you must have some reason for reading this book. Build on that. Even under the best of circumstances, you may get discouraged from time to time. If you need some inspiration, try the following:

- Visualize success. Create a sensory-rich image of your objective.[8] Use sight, sound, touch, smell, and taste.
- Relax. It may take a while to get there.
- Get right back at it. Even a small step in the right direction is better than no step at all.

Commitment

Once you have considered your motivation and understand that you are ready for action, you must establish a commitment, that is, a pledge of performance. You will take action and you pledge to yourself that you will perform. Intelligence, capacity, or ability are useless until they are applied to some objective. Since most accomplishments take time and require that some obstacles be overcome, it will be necessary to have sufficient commitment to get the whole job done.

How do you establish commitment? You must decide, in advance, that your goal is important enough to exclude other less important activities, and that you will overcome any obstacle that stands in your way.

Having established your goal based on your own priorities, reason, motivation, and commitment, you are now in need of what Killingsworth calls "rock-solid determination."[9] You may take your progress at a slow pace, but you will be like a bulldozer. Don't accept a stalemate or defeat. Remember, if it's important enough to do, it's important enough to do *right*. Steady forward progress is the key.

The objective here is to get through four stages, from (1) I *wish* this would happen (you examined why), to (2) I *want* this to happen (you established your goal), to (3) I *will make this happen* (you made a commitment), to (4) I *will make this happen, no matter what* (you are now determined).

Self-Discipline

In its simplest form, self-discipline is establishing a habit. Most people have little habits they perform each day. Some are better for us than others, but they are things that get done. Measurement is the link between an ordinary habit and continuous improvement. When you set a regular schedule for measuring results, you provide the opportunity to develop a habit. You then get a regular chance to congratulate yourself on your success, or take corrective action. Even if the results don't look good, they put you in a position to do something about it. Once measurement of carefully selected indicators gets to be a habit, you will be on the path to continuous improvement.

Vince Lombardi is reputed to have said "Practice doesn't make perfect. Perfect practice makes perfect." It is the continuous process of performance and measurement that enables us to accomplish great things. Use it.

Finally, it helps to have someone to talk to when things get tough. Seek the company of those who wish you to succeed.

Summary of the Process of Change

The key to continuous improvement is the understanding of the process of change. This process includes recognizing the need for change, then motivating yourself to change. We have discussed specific steps that you can take which will help you get off to a good start. The ancient Greeks had a saying: "Well begun: half done."

If you can get off to a good start by understanding what you want to change and why, by selecting only items that are worth your effort, by clearly visualizing your objectives, by establishing indicators by which you can measure results, and by doing first things first, the rest of the process will fall in line.

References

1. Tichy, Noel M., and Mary Anne Devanna. *The Transformational Leader.* New York: John Wiley & Sons, 1990, 68. This source provides the left-hand path of this diagram. The right-hand path is the result of application of quality improvement concepts to the process of change.

2. Rosander, A. C. *The Quest for Quality in Services.* Milwaukee: ASQC Quality Press, 1989, 143.

3. I heard this phrase first at the KAIZEN® Institute training, but the phrase itself has been around for a long time in psychological circles.

4. Taichi Ohno, of Toyota, is credited with this concept, which is covered in the Florida Power & Light Team Leader Training Course.

5. Jongaeward, Dorothy, ed. *Everybody Wins.* Reading, MA: Addison-Wesley, 1973, 142.

6. The phrase "what gets measured gets done" has been around for so long that it should probably be counted as quality improvement folklore. A diligent search has not produced a living quality professional who will take personal credit for coining the phrase.

7. Crosby, Philip B. *Quality Without Tears.* New York: New American Library, 1984, 59.

8. Deaton, Dennis R. *Visioneering: The Art of Power Goaling.* Chicago: Nightingale-Conant, 1988 (audiotape).

9. Killingsworth, Jim. (QUALTEC) 1989 interviews on the subject of quality management.

Suggested Reading

Crosby, Philip B. *Quality Without Tears.* New York: New American Library, 1984.

Deaton, Dennis R. *Visioneering: The Art of Power Goaling.* Chicago: Nightingale-Conant, 1988 (audiotape).

Gabor, Andrea. *The Man Who Discovered Quality.* New York: Random House, 1990.

Hansen, Mark Victor. *Future Diary.* Newport Beach, CA: Mark Victor Hansen Publishing Co., 1980.

Jongaeward, Dorothy, ed. *Everybody Wins.* Reading, MA: Addison-Wesley, 1973.

Juran, J. M. *Juran on Planning for Quality.* New York: Free Press, 1988.

Walton, Mary. *The Deming Management Method.* New York: Pedigree Books, 1986.

Three

STRUCTURED PROBLEM SOLVING

In Chapter 2, a distinction was drawn between the process of personal change and the act of structured problem solving. The reason for drawing this distinction is that the selection of a focus area is critical to the effective use of one's time. It is possible to be an effective problem solver and yet feel frustrated because the results do not appear important to you. By making use of the analysis presented in the previous chapter, which I will call wishbone analysis (after the shape of the diagram), we can avoid this pitfall.

On the negative side, if we have not completed the wishbone analysis before starting structured problem solving, we run the risk of losing momentum before the project is completed, or completing the project but not feeling gratified.

STRUCTURED PROBLEM SOLVING, THE PROCESS

Quality improvement literature abounds with methods of structured problem solving. This presentation blends the ideas of many creative thinkers. Those whose ideas have been used extensively have consented to allow the use of their original materials, while others have been acknowledged at the end of each chapter.

The basic process, shown in Figure 3.1, was drawn primarily from Mary Walton (Deming), Juran and Frank Gryna, and A. C. Rosander. For practical applications, extensive reference has been drawn from the programs of Florida Power and Light and ALCOA. Special thanks go to John Batcheller of Florida Power and Light, and Bob Kohm of ALCOA for providing research materials.

We'll be taking a two-stage approach to discussing structured problem solving. In Chapter 3, we will discuss the seven steps conceptually, with examples but very little detail. In Chapter 4, we will discuss the tools with lots of detail and more examples.

STEP ONE—PROBLEM IDENTIFICATION

Identify the need for change, select the vital few, narrow the field to most important one.

STEP TWO—PROBLEM ANALYSIS

Analyze the problem from many points of view in order to identify the root cause.

STEP THREE—EVALUATION AND PLANNING

Set the goal and direction, generate potential actions, evaluate and select actions, develop an action plan, refine indicators.

STEP FOUR—DATA COLLECTION

Collect data according to the indicators.

STEP FIVE—DATA INTERPRETATION

Determine if the data indicate progress or if rethinking is required.

STEP SIX—ACTION

Conduct a trial implementation and continue to monitor data.

STEP SEVEN—APPRAISAL/FUTURE PLANS

Determine if data show improvement, then continue with implementation or move on to another project.

FIGURE 3.1 Structured problem-solving steps

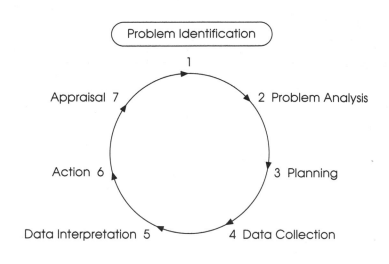

FIGURE 3.2 Step one—problem identification

STEP ONE—PROBLEM IDENTIFICATION

Problem identification is an ongoing process. From day to day, we are constantly identifying and prioritizing problems and opportunities. The question is, which ones are worthy of attention? Managing the process of change on a personal level facilitates the problem identification phase. Because we now have a framework within which we have reviewed our problems and opportunities and focused on the important issue, we are prepared to begin the structured problem-solving process. Also, because we are working on the right issue, we know that the time invested in the process will be well spent. Finally, because we have created a sensory-rich image of the positive outcome of our efforts, it will be easier to see the project through.

Now let's look at the individual matter selected, keeping in mind that the process of change is always in action. At any step in this seven-step process, we may want to consider our personal reactions to the new discoveries to ensure that we stay on track.

Since most of us spend part of our time at home and the other part at work, we might have two things going on at once: personal objectives and business objectives. Let's take one of each through the problem identification phase.

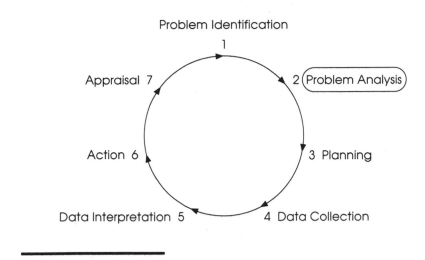

FIGURE 3.3 Step two—problem analysis

Problem Identification—Issues

Following through with the work already done in Chapter 2, we have identified getting in shape as the most important problem. Three indicators considered include weight, waist dimension in inches, and muscle tone. Our mental image of the end product is a lean, energetic body.

On the business side, let's imagine that we work in the inside sales group for a large company. Recently, the volume of telephone calls has gotten so great that we can't handle them effectively and customers are complaining. Our vision of the end product is satisfied customers (no complaints) and a pleasant work environment in which we look forward to coming to work in the morning and do not leave in a state of total exhaustion at the end of the day.

Throughout this chapter, we will develop these examples, taking each through the seven-step process of structured problem solving.

STEP TWO—PROBLEM ANALYSIS

This is the stage in which we pick the problem apart, using quality improvement tools (described later in this book) to identify the "root cause" of the problem. The root cause is the ultimate cause, that if corrected will result in the elimination of the problem (for example, the disease, not the symptom).

We have already used the tools of checklist and brainstorming in step one. Root causes may be easier to identify if you apply the tools mentioned in Chapter 4 (for example, flowcharts and cause-and-effect diagrams). But on a personal basis, the Five Whys should get you to the root cause. The problem analysis step need not be long and complicated, but must not be skipped. The danger in skipping this step is that you could go to great length to apply a solution to the wrong thing.

As an example, let's take our number one item from Figure 2.3, getting in shape. It's not too difficult to find a typical cause for excess weight: eating too much. By the same token, an individual may have a specific medical problem of which he or she is unaware. In order to do the job of weight reduction right, the possible causes of excess weight should be evaluated and the actual root cause dealt with.

In order to keep this uncomplicated, we will assume that we have had a complete medical examination and at the recommendation of our doctor, we eliminate the eating of pies. Applying the Crosby zero defects approach our target is to eat no pies.[1] Eating even one pie does not meet our requirements. Our specific indicators are number of pies eaten and weight in pounds.

Many problems are more complicated than this and will require the use of a variety of tools to reach a thorough analysis. On the other hand, many problems that at first seem complicated can actually be reduced to extremely simple root causes. If your root cause seems complicated, it is a good bet that you haven't really found your root cause. Look deeper until your cause is clear and understandable.

To illustrate, let's go to the customer service department, mentioned previously. We used brainstorming to identify a variety of specific customer needs, and developed a checklist to keep track of requests handled and complaints. We used simple hash marks to count each event as it occurred. When we met to look at the actual data, it turned out that the hash marks showed customer complaints were due to lack of service and jumped when any one person in the group is away from his or her desk. We can now use

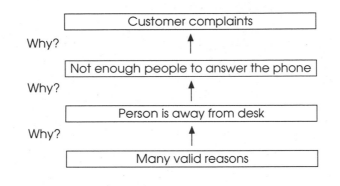

FIGURE 3.4 Customer complaint flowchart

the Five Whys to look deeper. The results of this investigation can be shown on a simple flowchart, as shown in Figure 3.4.

Actually, this flowchart is backward. Let's look at it from bottom to top, and restate the problem. Many valid reasons cause a person to be away from his or her desk. This reduces total capacity, resulting in customer complaints. The root causes of customer complaints are the "many valid reasons." If we have looked at all the options in this oversimplified example, looking into the "many valid reasons" will lead us to reduced customer complaints. If the checklist had shown complaints due to poor service, rather than lack of service, our direction would have been different.

One final warning: We all have a tendency to skip to solutions when we first see a glimmer of understanding. Resist this temptation. Identifying and selecting solutions comes later. Stick to identifying the root cause in this step. When you are certain that you have identified the root cause, you are ready for step three.

DEVELOPING AN ACTION PLAN

Ever hear the expression "don't put the cart before the horse"? Of course. Like most simple concepts, this idea has broad practical use. Every project can be done in a variety of ways, but there is usually one particular way that is easier, takes less time, is more economical, or better than the rest for some other reason. That's the one we're looking for.

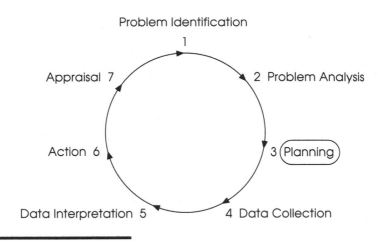

FIGURE 3.5 Step three—planning

Imagine what it would be like to do everything you do in half the time or at half the cost. Think of the impact on your energy level, not to mention your pocketbook.

What we want to do is lay out the individual tasks in your project in the order in which they must be started and finished. You can then consider the alternatives and develop the best plan.

Taking our weight loss example, we might plan to start with pies, measuring our weight reduction until it was stable for one month. At that time, if we have not reached our objective, we may have a list of other goodies ranked in order of decreasing calories, which would be systematically removed from the diet, each time looking for a four-week period of no change. Again, this may seem overly methodical for a simple problem, yet it is important to get into the habit of setting goals and measuring results.

When you plan, use a pencil with an eraser because you will probably want to make many changes before you are finished.

Review your chart, which shows the order of actions you will take, to make sure that everything is included. A small oversight could have a large effect. Taking our example, if you put a low-calorie item at the top of the list, you would waste four weeks with little or no results. When you reach an impasse, put the chart down for a while, then pick it up again later for a fresh look.

You may see from the chart that there are certain critical points at which you want to check your indicators. You will notice that certain things must be done in order, and some not. Those things which must be done in sequence, upon which the whole project depends, are called the "critical path."[2]

Returning to our customer service group, we had identified the valid reasons, which included scheduled breaks, bathroom visits, and visits to other departments for complaint resolution. The order of action was determined as follows:

1. Log each time you leave the work area, stating the reason.
2. Summarize the logs and use statistics to analyze the results.
3. Take corrective action based on results.

These items must be done in this order. This is a critical path. Say, for example, Robby observes that his scheduled break is during a busy time. Before completing step two, he reschedules his break. Without knowing it, Julie reschedules her break, too. Unfortunately, both are now out of the work area at the same time, making the problem worse. Robby and Julie can do many other things in their daily work, but this particular project must be taken in this order only. The seven-step process itself is a critical path. You can observe, collect data, think, talk to your customers, and be creative all along the way, but if you want the process to work, you must take each step relating to this project in turn.

Contingency Planning

No plan is complete without a contingency plan. What do you do if your plan goes wrong? The importance of the issue will determine how much time you spend on contingency planning. We can't guarantee in advance that a project will unfold exactly as we expect. It makes sense to give some advance thought to likely alternatives, and to what our responses might be.

Using our weight example: What would we do if our weight does not decrease when we stop eating pies?

DATA COLLECTION

So far, we have identified the need for change, analyzed the problem, found the root cause, planned the corrective action, and we

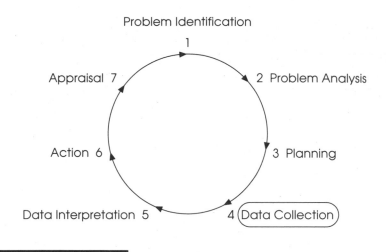

FIGURE 3.6 Step four—data collection

are now ready to accumulate data. We have elected to use a simple piece of paper taped to the bathroom mirror to monitor our weight on a daily basis. A simple chart makes it easy to track your progress. We have also put in a column to indicate a day without pies. Remember, we are trying to establish a measurement habit. Since our indicator of change was one month at a stable weight, we are looking for that pattern to develop. We may also see if there is a relationship between the lack of pies and the reduction of weight.

When we reach that point, we will review our situation. Figure 3.7 shows the results of our effort.

DATA INTERPRETATION

Now that we have developed a regular pattern of collecting data and have reached a level of standardization (one month at a stable weight), we are prepared to analyze our situation. Although this may seem like a lot of trouble for just losing a few pounds, remember that this same process will be used over and over again, so it's important to understand the basics first.

Some experts might argue that we were incorrect in taking *any* action before we had begun to collect our beginning data. Others

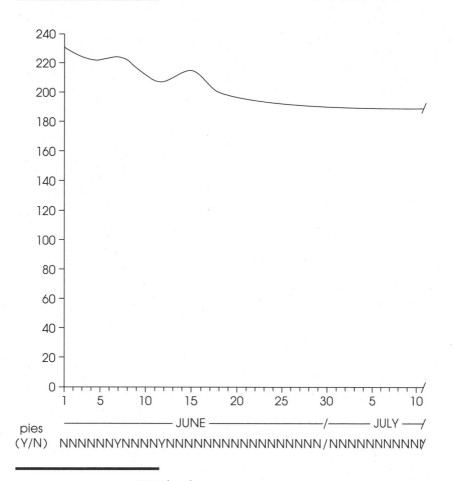

FIGURE 3.7 Weight chart

would argue that you should not waste time if you already know a corrective action with a high chance of success. In this case, we did the obvious (eliminating pies) right away. As a result, we were able not only to achieve results sooner, but also get a feel for some of the practical aspects of our project.

Our first observation is that we need only one indicator, not two. We will discontinue the counting of pies. We've just cut our work in half.

Our second observation is that we need to plan a target weight to define the goal in terms of the indicator. Remember, our image of success had nothing to do with weight, it had to do with

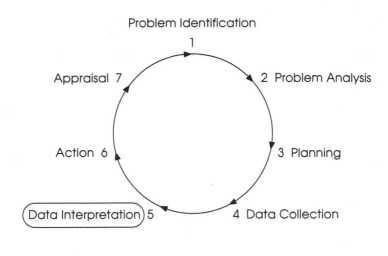

FIGURE 3.8 Step five—data interpretation

appearance. Yet weight can be used as a convenient substitute until a better indicator is developed. After consulting the medical charts, we find that our target weight is 175 pounds. We notice the chart is not fine enough to show our actual measurement. So, we'll redraw our chart to show 1-pound changes.

Finally, we found that foregoing the pies will only get us to 190 pounds. Further analysis will show us where to go from here. Without getting too scientific, we identify a number of other things to do, including diet and exercise, which will lead us closer to the goal.

Using Figure 3.9, the original chart revised to show 1-pound increments and to emphasize only the weight range of immediate concern, we are ready to go on to the next step: action.

ACTION

Based on our data, we found that more changes were in order. We have selected exercise as the next step. Since we are aware of our personal habits (and because we haven't read the chapter on tools

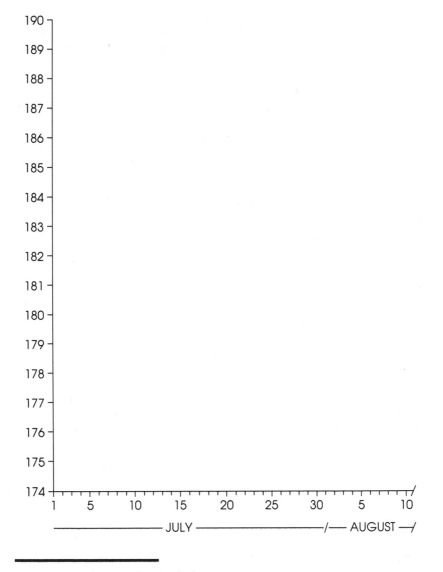

FIGURE 3.9 Revised chart

yet), we are comfortable with that decision. We have modified our chart to show only the range we are concerned with, and in 1-pound increments. The action consists of one 15-minute session every day. Since we view this as our most important issue, we have

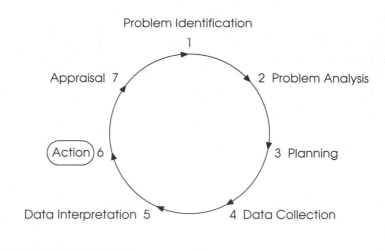

FIGURE 3.10 Step six—action

no problem mustering the discipline necessary to exercise 15 min-utes each day, without exception.

The target has been added to our chart (Figure 3.11) to em-phasize the importance of and distance to our goal. The figure also shows the results of this phase.

APPRAISAL

In this last step, we have two objectives:

1. To evaluate, as factually as possible, our perfor-mance on this project.
2. To determine if we are finished yet.

Upon review of our progress to date, we find that we have not yet achieved our target, but are still making steady progress. Based on our indicators and firm target, we have not finished.

Priorities can change from time to time, so at this point we will allow ourselves to reconsider our priorities. Perhaps the progress to this point is acceptable. Perhaps the process is sufficiently under control, and we have enough additional energy to take on a second project. This is not recommended if you are still struggling with

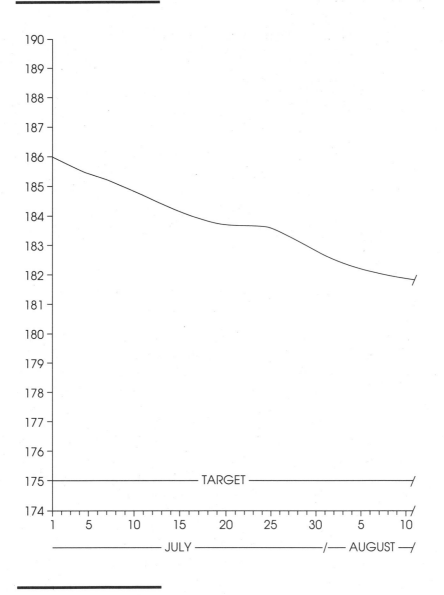

FIGURE 3.11 Revised chart

project number one. Most important, if we want to build a winning habit, we're better off sticking to project number one until
our objective has been reached to our absolute satisfaction, looking neither right nor left until the job is done.

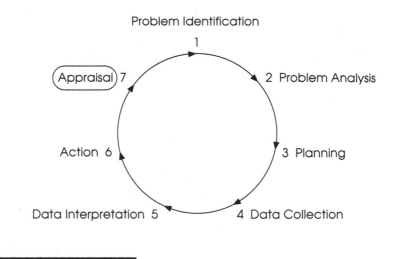

FIGURE 3.12 Step seven—appraisal

When we have achieved our target, according to our measurable indicators, we still have the same basic question, perhaps phrased in a different way: Do we want to tighten our controls, and repeat the process once more around the seven-step cycle? Or are we ready to go on to another issue?

Having completed the entire process, from problem identification to appraisal, we are prepared to embark on the journey of continuous improvement. Practiced effectively, this process feeds itself because each improvement eliminates wasted time and energy and improves our focus on the important issues, making each effort in turn more and more successful.

Using the checklist in Figure 3.13 we can check our performance at each step in the cycle. In future projects, we can keep a running checklist to ensure that we have completed each step before advancing to the next step.

Customer Service Revisited

Let's return to our customer service group where we left several things undone. They needed some different tools to complete their process. Where we left off, they had identified reasons for being away from the work area. They monitored their reasons for being

STEP	INDICATOR	RESULTS
Identification	Created a mental picture Established an indicator	
Problem Analysis	Identified the root cause(s)	
Planning	Generated potential actions Evaluated actions Developed action plan	
Data Collection	Monitor indicator	
Data Interpretation	Do data support your original ideas?	
Action	Took corrective action Monitored indicator	
Appraisal	Tightened controls or moved on to another project.	

FIGURE 3.13 Process checklist

away for a period of one week. Looking at the data from several points of view was very helpful.

When each person charted their own reasons, everything looked perfectly normal to them. When all occurrences were totalled, then presented by category, a different picture was presented. They found the data as follows:

REASON	TIMES	MINUTES
Scheduled breaks	15	900
Bathroom visits	20	200
Visits to other departments	5	300
Group total	40	1400
Total time available		12,000
Members of group—5		

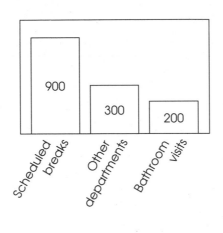

FIGURE 3.14 Basic Pareto chart

By consolidating their notes, these individuals found power in the group data. They decided that the most important indicator was minutes away from the desk rather than occurrences. They then put the reasons in rank order, and charted them, as shown in Figure 3.14.

The graphic presentation of these data enhances our ability to communicate numbers in perspective. It clearly shows the dominant position of scheduled breaks as the source of time out of the work group.

The individual, in this case, could not solve the problem alone. He needed the help of others. Yet, the final solution involved individual commitment. The solution they chose was to readjust their break and lunch schedules to avoid busy telephone times. They continued to monitor complaints, and found that they were reduced. Since there were still complaints, they decided to go through the seven-step process again and work on the remaining problems.

SUMMARY OF THE SEVEN-STEP PROCESS

When we talk about quality improvement and the process of change, we are talking about two processes that support one another. You cannot improve quality without making some change. When we create change, we usually have some improvement in mind. We must understand the process of change in order to get started on a quality improvement project. We must understand that there must be a reason to change, and we must then motivate ourselves to take action. This must occur in the beginning of the quality improvement process. We cannot complete the process of change without taking meaningful action. Steps two through six of the quality improvement process offer a structured way to organize and take appropriate actions. Finally, we will never feel successful unless we can see tangible results. Step seven gives us a structure within which we can review our results. If we have not accomplished our goals, we can identify new corrective actions based upon our checklist, get back into the process, and move forward until we do get results.

Once you have become familiar with this process, you will realize that the only important barriers are the ones you place upon yourself, both knowingly and unknowingly. Someone once told me, "Quality improvement will change your life." He was right. In the next section, we will discuss some of the typical obstacles you are likely to encounter on your journey to quality improvement through personal change.

References

1. Crosby, Philip B. *Quality Without Tears*. New York: New American Library, 1984, 74.

2. Budnick, Frank S., Richard Mojena, and Thomas E. Vollman. *Principles of Operations Research for Management*. Homewood, IL: Richard D. Irwin, 1977, 543. This includes a more specific definition.

Suggested Reading

Ingle, Sud. *In Search of Perfection*. Englewood Cliffs, NJ: Prentice-Hall, 1985.

Rosander, A. C. *The Quest for Quality in Services*. Milwaukee: ASQC Quality Press, 1989.

Four

OVERCOMING
OBSTACLES

So far, we have described the five-stage process of change and seven-step structured problem-solving quality improvement approach as applied to personal change. Between the two, we have gone from initial goal setting through appraisal. It takes experience to get this process working for you, and your first few efforts may take more than one try. One thing is certain: You will encounter obstacles. The way you deal with these obstacles is an important part of your self-improvement process. It's not possible to predict exactly what your obstacles will be, but there are some common ones that have been identified by research and practice. Being prepared for the known obstacles will give you a better chance of overcoming them. These obstacles fall into two categories: the personal and organizational. We will discuss the personal obstacles here and the organizational obstacles in later chapters.

GOAL SETTING

Think back to the three basic concepts of continuous improvement: identifying a problem, motivating yourself to do something about it, and taking action. The balance with which you select goals is critical to your success because of its link to your own internal reward system. We all like the satisfaction of accomplishment. Some of us have a deep-seated need for regular reward, such as applause to an actor. Others can engage in multiyear projects, and can thrive without the day-to-day praise. It is important to know how often you need to experience success or completion. By taking this important factor into consideration, you can select projects and set goals that strike the right balance for you. If a project looks too big for your personal style to accommodate, try breaking it up into smaller parts. In that way, you can experience completion and reward yourself at the end of each part.

PACE

Setting a pace for yourself and the project is also important. Your personal, long-term pace is the speed at which you can keep working, day in and day out, without getting exhausted or discouraged. There is another pace which is equally important. It is the pace at which the project itself must run in order for other involved parties to stay interested in it. If you are working with others, you must find a way to achieve the necessary project pace while meeting your own needs. This may mean assembling a team that divides the load according to the individual paces of its members.

THE GREAT AMERICAN MYTH

Early in our married life, my wife, Diane, made the statement, "Nothing worthwhile comes easily." She was right. No effort is trouble-free. Crosby says it a little differently: "Quality is free, but it is not a gift."[1]

The great American myth is that there is a quick fix, an easy solution to most problems. Not true. Most problems have accumulated gradually over time and involve a variety of elements. To turn a situation around will take time. Even on a personal level, you may have to make many small changes to achieve a significant improvement. If you avoid the great myth of the quick fix, you will have avoided a major pitfall.

APATHY AND INDIFFERENCE

Thinking about change is the first step in eliminating apathy, indifference, and other negative thoughts. One approach to dealing with the negatives is to establish a habit that will carry you through in spite of them. Even the smallest project can have its irritating moments. Much of this has to do with personal style. A system of self-discipline is required. In its simplest form, self-discipline is nothing more than a habit. We're trying to build a habit so strong that it carries us through all the little ups and downs at a more or less constant pace. We may wish to deviate from this pattern once it is established, but only for a specific time and specific purpose. The measurement process is the key to developing your habit. Once you have become accustomed to measuring results on a regular basis, you will have both your discipline and an opportunity to get regular doses of success.

FEAR

Fear is a normal part of life. Even if we do nothing, we may still fear the consequences. The trick to handling fear is to deal with it, not avoid it. Fears tend to fall into two general categories: fear of failure and fear of success.

Fear of Failure

This fear is based on fear of the consequences of failures, not the actual facts. Failure itself is really an internal process, because it is defined as not meeting *your* objectives. Things people typically associate with failures include loss of income, loss of prestige, and loss of friendships.

Fear of Success

Fear of success is a little more tricky. Psychologists haven't found a complete answer to this one. It seems that many people are afraid that success will change them in some way to make them different than they were. Their friends and loved ones will no longer love them because they have become different. The fallacy of this argument is that you *don't* have to be a different person that people won't like. If anything, people will want to associate themselves with your personal success. Some people have spent years in therapy to overcome this problem, without success. Some people are tremendously successful without any help at all. The bottom line is that if you follow this or any other process to accomplish your goals, stick to your process, and monitor your results, you will probably be successful. Don't get dragged down by worrying about when you will get there or what you will be like when you arrive.

If you have done a good job of selecting the right issues to work on, the potential benefits will by far outweigh the risks. Allow yourself to experience the fear, but don't let it paralyze you.

THE PROCESS

Armed with an awareness of potential obstacles, we can apply structured thinking and analysis to almost any situation we face. This will not necessarily make success easy, but it will almost certainly make it easier. The remainder of this book will make more sense if we consider that our lives are a combination of many interacting systems or processes. Most of what we do is devoted to making these processes work for us. Armed with a solid process, we can make improvement an everyday thing. Let's start with the definition of process; a series of acts aimed at a single end.

A process has three key elements:

1. Inputs, things provided at the beginning of the process, to which the process is applied.
2. Actions, the things that are done to the inputs to change them.
3. Outputs, the results of the actions, which then usually feed some other *process*.

Each step in a process can be considered in light of the types of inputs provided. One convenient way to remember types of inputs is the four *M*'s, to which I add one *I*.

1. Man, or people.
2. Methods, or procedures.
3. Machine, including tools, computers, etc.
4. Materials.
5. Information, which can control the whole process.

Implementation problems can be traced to one of these areas. Your obstacles will fall into at least one of these areas.

People

Until now, the "people" in this book has been you. Later in the book, we will deal with others in a group environment. One handy technique for managing your personal process is the in-basket exercise.

In the in-basket exercise, the student tries his or her hand at dealing with a steady stream of activities. The student prioritizes, sorts, and takes actions. There is a method for dealing with the in-basket. Since many of our activities can be viewed as a perpetual in-basket, this method can be a valuable tool. It has to do with queuing theory, or theory of lines, which is discussed in detail in the tools section.

The basic situation is this: it takes time to prioritize your in-basket. This time is frequently wasted because you must work each item anyway. The most effective solution to this problem is to act on each item in turn, devoting only the appropriate amount of attention to it (based on your priorities) and handling each item only once. All other possible solutions are less effective. You may say, "I don't have time to work on all these items, so I must prioritize." This may be true on a temporary basis, but it will not do as a permanent solution. Prioritization will never solve a capacity problem. If you do not have time to handle the incoming work right the first time, then you must get help, put more hours on the task, or figure out a way to do it faster.

Once you have mastered the concept of the in-basket exercise, you will have a habit of managing your tasks in an organized way. You may handle certain items at certain times of day. You may have a tickle file from which you work. Whatever technique you use, you must use it religiously. It is the strength of this habit which will pull you through many a slump (and we all have them).

Fear of failure will decrease automatically as you become more comfortable with your system. If you have followed your system, you won't fail. You will develop a winning habit and it will be hard to break. If you are having doubts, take a moment and visualize success. Create a mental picture of what it will look like when you have achieved your goal. The clearer this image, the more strength it will have in carrying you through the ups and downs.

Methods (Procedures)

Just like our in-basket exercise, every task has a procedure which works on a continuing basis to ensure that the task is completed correctly. Many failings to act result from lack of having a set procedure. If you're not sure what the procedure is or should be, write it down. Many of the tools discussed in the next chapter will help define and improve procedures. The process of writing out a procedure gives the opportunity to view it at close range. You see things that you may have missed all along. As a result, you will find opportunities to save yourself time or money.

Machine

"Masaaki Imai, in his KAIZEN® course, gives an example of a case where a Japanese company purchased wire machines from a Belgian company. The machines were of the same design as the Belgian counterpart was using. During the machine installation and subsequent operations the Japanese employees suggested hundreds of improvements. This resulted in the machines outperforming the Belgian machines by 300%. Anything can be improved. Don't limit your thinking."[2]

Materials

The same points made about machines can be duplicated here. Keep an open mind; consider alternatives.

Information

Many problems occur because, at some stage in a process, necessary and sufficient information is not available to do the job right. The person doing the job may or may not be aware that he or she doesn't have the information. If a process is to work as designed, the correct information must be present at each step along the way.

In planning, we frequently do not have complete information. It can be argued that we never have complete information. We must learn to make value judgments regarding the amount of information required to meet our needs on each occasion. We must find out how much information we need, then acquire it and take action. Do not get hung up on accumulating an endless stream of confirming data. You can frequently get a lot of information out of just a few points. The further you get from planning and the closer to actually doing, the more concrete your information needs to be.

Do It

One of the basic principles of KAIZEN®, or continuing improvement, as taught by Imai, is the phrase "do it," or in Japanese "*ya re.*"

What this means is that the problem-solving or continuous improvement process need not take a long time. Some people and organizations get hung up on taking every decision down to the very finest degree. The result is frequently that nothing gets done: paralysis by analysis.

Imai points out that you can make many improvements by problem solving right in the workplace at the point where the action occurs, and implement the solution right away. Doing this effectively requires complete command of the seven-step process. Yet once it is learned and practiced, the seven step-process can be used quite rapidly at any time.

Your first few tries at using this method may take a while, in terms of days or weeks. As you become more comfortable with the order of events, you will be able to go through the steps in minutes or even seconds.

If you already know what you must do, then for your own sake do it now. *Ya re.* Measure your results, take corrective action, and continue to move forward.

SUMMARY

The continuous improvement process is divided into three areas: identifying the need for change, securing motivation to change, and taking action. Obstacles will be met and must be overcome. The most important obstacles are personal ones and must be overcome on a personal basis. By applying tools and techniques that have been field-tested, we can make it easier to get past our personal obstacles. By knowing what obstacles we are likely to face, and handling them in an organized way, we can minimize the impact of negative feelings on our overall progress.

Both quality improvement and the process of change are first and foremost personal processes. Neither one is somebody else's job, it is *our* job. We must master both quality improvement and the process of change on a personal basis before we try to bring them into someone else's world.

References

1. Crosby, Philip B. *Quality Is Free*. New York: McGraw-Hill, 1979, 1.

2. Imai, Masaaki. Basic and Advanced KAIZEN® Course, KAIZEN® Institute, Austin, TX, Spring 1990, and subsequent interviews with Mr. Imai.

Suggested Reading

Crosby, Philip B. *Quality Is Free*. New York: McGraw-Hill, 1979.

Imai, Masaaki. *Kaizen*. New York: Random House, 1986.

Jeffers, Susan. *Feel the Fear and Do It Anyway*. Chicago: Nightingale-Conant, 1988 (audiotape).

Starker, Steven. *Parathink: The Paranoia of Everyday Life*. Far Hills, NJ: New Horizon Press, 1986.

Section Two

_____

QUALITY IMPROVEMENT TOOLS

_____

Five

PERSONAL CHANGE: FROM THEORY TO PRACTICE

The approach taken so far can be summarized in the following three sentences:

1. The process of change (like charity) begins "at home," with the individual.
2. Understanding the stages of change can help us deal with personal changes in a constructive way.
3. The seven-step quality improvement process can be applied to personal change, both in a private setting and at work. This can be accomplished at least for those things under our direct control.

Continuing in a stepwise progression:

4. Specific quality improvement tools can be applied at each step in the seven-step process. These tools either help us understand, quantify, or control the process.
5. Later in the book, we will explore methods of expanding this process to situations beyond ourselves.

The three concepts shown in Figure 5.1 interact to accomplish continuous improvement.

EVERYDAY QUALITY TOOLS

There is a wealth of information about quality tools available to the serious student of quality improvement programs. This chapter

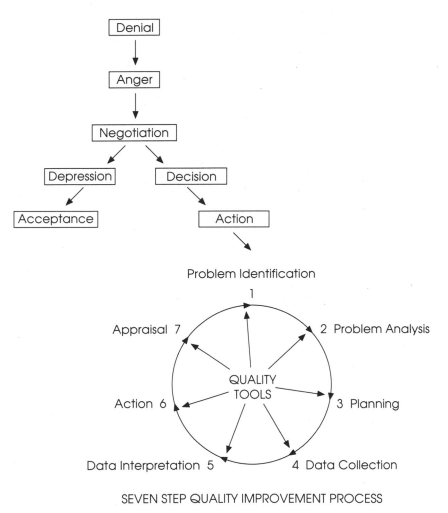

FIGURE 5.1 Quality improvement, quality tools, and the process of change

is devoted to providing a basic understanding of the range of quality tools available to you, so that they can be explained in detail in Chapter 6. Examples of each will be given so that you can apply them immediately. At the end of Chapter 6 is a list of references for more specific background and information on quality improvement tools.

When you first start to improve something, you will probably be making a gross change, like from having no plan at all to having a simple plan in place. Say, for example, you handle your in-basket on a first-in, first-out basis at 9:00 every morning. When you've been at it for awhile, you may have the need to expand your knowledge as you refine your activities to ever-tighter circles of control.

There are four types of tools: conceptual, quantitative, control or tracking, and appraisal. Each can be applied as needed in any step of the process. By understanding the step in the quality process and the uses of the tools, you can select the tool that will serve you best the first time, and save yourself a lot of extra work.

TYPES OF QUALITY TOOLS

The quality tools we will discuss include the seven basic tools: cause-and-effect diagram, Pareto chart, check sheet, histogram, scatter diagram, control chart, and graphs. We will also include tools from self-improvement literature and a few from other sources.

Because of the nature of the seven-step quality process, you will expect to apply certain tools at each individual step. For example, brainstorming is one of the first tools you will use and one of the last. The quantitative tools, like histograms and Pareto charts, are used throughout the process, but in different places than brainstorming. The monitoring or tracking tools are used once you have developed a plan of action. Finally, appraisal is used once you have completed a project to evaluate the whole process and make adjustments where needed. As you become more experienced in the quality process, you may find that you are using appraisal continually (you can't stop).

Figure 5.2 shows the tools we will describe. Remember that since improvement is a continuous process, your use of tools may overlap. This chart is a guide to help you focus on the tools which will likely be of assistance as you work through a situation. In the next chapter, we will give a background for each tool and some examples of personal and business uses.

CONCEPT DEVELOPMENT TOOLS

The list

Brainstorming

Five Whys

Visualization

Flowchart

Objective statement

Prioritizing

QUANTITATIVE TOOLS

Statistics

Theory of lines

Ishikawa or cause-and-effect diagram

Pareto chart

CONTROL OR TRACKING TOOLS

Control chart

Gantt chart

Critical path chart

Decision matrix

APPRAISAL TOOLS

Checklist

The story

FIGURE 5.2 Types of quality improvement tools

PLANNING STAGE	ACTIVITIES	TOOLS APPLIED
1. Problem Identification	Identify needs Consider options Narrow the field Develop objective	Brainstorming List Five Whys Visualization
2. Analysis	Look at situation from many points-of-view Determine root cause	Graphic tools
3. Planning	Set goal Generate potential Actions Develop action plans	Gantt chart Barriers and aids Cost of quality Contingencies Decision matrix
4. Data Collection	Plot indicators Monitor progress	Graphic tools
5. Data Interpretation	Interpret results	Graphic tools
6. Action	Do it now	Objective statement Brainstorming Decision matrix Five Whys
7. Appraisal	Compare results to objectives	Objective statement Graphic tools The story

FIGURE 5.3 Tools and their applications

Checklist

Flowchart

Fishbone diagram

Pie chart

Bar graph

Histogram

Pareto chart

Scatter diagram

Control chart

Note: These graphic tools can be used throughout the process.

FIGURE 5.4 Summary of graphic tools

Suggested Reading

Alessandra, Tony, and Jim Cathcart. *Relationship Strategies*. Chicago: Nightingale-Conant, 1984.

Deaton, Dennis R. *Visioneering: The Art of Power Goaling*. Chicago: Mind Masters Institute, Inc., Nightingale-Conant (audiotape).

Jeffers, Susan. *Feel the Fear and Do It Anyway*. Chicago: Nightingale-Conant, 1988 (audiotape).

Peters, T., and R. Townsend. *Excellence in the Organization*. Chicago: Nightingale-Conant, 1990 (audiotape).

"The Tools of Quality." *Quality Progress 6–12*, Vol. 23 (June 1990-December 1990).

Ziglar, Zig. *Selling Your Way to the Top*. Chicago: Nightingale-Conant, 1990 (audiotape).

Six

PRACTICAL APPLICATIONS

Whether in our business or personal lives, we can view our thoughts and actions as an accumulation of processes. Individual actions can be controlled or improved. Even more powerful results occur when we control or improve a process, because we may use the same process in many areas of our lives at the same time. The benefit is multiplied by the number of times the process is used. The more basic this process is to us, the more power we gain by improving it. In fact, there are so many opportunities for improvement that we need a way to keep track of our options.

1. There is a single improvement to a single action.
2. We can generalize this improvement and apply it to other individual actions.
3. We can abstract the improvement and apply it to a whole class of actions. In other words, we can standardize.
4. We can peel the onion one more layer and move the process upstream to a more basic level of our person. This process then becomes more universal.

In summary, we can produce both vertical and horizontal integration of our improvements, broadening our horizons as we go.

The options are summarized in graphic form in Figure 6.1. We can achieve both vertical and horizontal integration in our personal quality improvements.

In addition to the information in Figure 6.1, each element in the example can be passed along to other people through effective communication.

How can we control such a variety of opportunities? Through the use of the objective statement and cost-benefit analysis, also

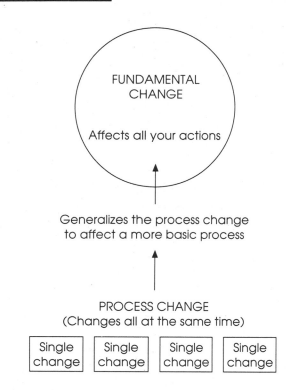

FIGURE 6.1 Hierarchy of improvement options

known as cost of quality or cost of poor quality (depending on your point of view).

Everything flows from the objective statement. It may be a highly focused statement addressed to a specific situation, or it may be a broad, comprehensive life overview statement. Whichever is chosen, it is likely that the quality and scope of the results will match the quality and scope of the objective statement.

For example, let's consider Fuller's objective statement, which was framed in the form of a question.

> What could I effectively do . . . that could not be done by great nations or great private enterprise to lastingly improve the physical protection and support of all human lives, at the same time removing undesirable restraints and improving individual initiatives of any and all humans aboard our planet earth?

This statement is at the same time vague and specific. Let's analyze it.

Who?	R. Buckminster Fuller (self)
What?	Personal accomplishment Improve physical protection and support of all human lives Remove undesirable restraints Improve individual initiatives Not doable by organizations
When?	Lastingly (permanent improvements) Intention appears to be immediate
Where?	Undefined
Why?	Personal reasons
How?	Undefined

By leaving the "where" open, Fuller removed a (undesirable?) constraint . . . he could do this anywhere. The "how" relates to the question itself. It is a matter of history that Fuller accomplished a great deal, although he is perhaps best known for the invention of the geodesic dome. All the other blanks are filled in from the start. Although his training prior to the age of 32 might well have taken him in other directions, it seems clear that from that point forward his life work revolved around his objective statement.

Cost-benefit analysis has been a part of business decision-making for a long time. Yet decision makers sometimes have a hard time dealing with intangible benefits (such as motivation, goodwill, or customer service) on a cost/benefit basis. Yet to make an improvement stick in the long run, it must be viewed as beneficial by the users, customers, and management. The "benefit" may be in currency or in other measurable forms.

The same concept is true on a personal basis. It costs money to do things, for example, attend courses or buy books, or purchase measuring equipment. But money is not our only resource. We apply other personal resources, like time and energy, to projects. Something of value must come back to return that investment to your satisfaction. Since money is easy to quantify, the option chosen is frequently to express the value of nonmonetary resources in dollars. This process allows for comparison of various uses of resources. That's where cost of quality comes in. Keep in mind that this process can be reversed. In other words, we can also express monetary costs in terms of the amount and type of resources that money can purchase.

Let's assume for a moment that we adopt Fuller's objective statement for our own use. Where do we go from here?

We've already considered the process of change, and the requirements of that process, in earlier chapters. In order to focus on specific application of tools, let's assume that we have passed through the stages as follows:

1. Denial: We no longer deny that many things require improvement. We no longer deny that we are world citizens.

2. Anger: We accept our anger, which is caused by frustration and feelings of powerlessness to produce change.

3. Negotiation: We open ourselves to the process of change.

4. Decision: We have made a commitment to action.

5. Action: We are beginning with an objective statement.

Now let's get specific and apply some quality improvement tools.

CONCEPTUAL TOOLS

Having established a broad-based objective statement, it is now time to get specific. If our goal is too broad, it can inhibit our progress. We can use brainstorming, the list, visualization, the objective statement, the Five Whys, and the flowchart to provide a specific objective statement that is capable of immediate action. We will also provide sufficient incentive that we will execute that objective statement, participating in the rewards along the way.

Conceptual tools are used to get started with the process of change, to generate ideas, to narrow them down, and to provide an objective statement that will serve as the guidepost for the later steps. They can also be used within the other process steps as needed.

Brainstorming

Although brainstorming was discussed earlier, it is useful to review a few key points.

Use brainstorming when you want to generate ideas. Think about the process for a minute. In an individual or group environment, ideas don't flow when you stop to criticize them or when you inhibit them. So the first rule of brainstorming is to allow no negatives to creep into the process. Stay positive.

Write every idea down. If the process is really working, they will come fast and furious. For personal brainstorming, a notepad is good enough. For group efforts, an easel is handy because you can write big enough for everybody to see. Tape the charts to the wall, allowing one idea to feed another. Write down all ideas.

That's all there is to it. Try it some time. Twenty to thirty good ideas in a short session is not unusual. One good session will give you enough to work on for a year, five years, or even a lifetime—it's the development of the ideas that takes time.

Let's apply the brainstorming process to the objective statement, which I will call for now the Fuller objective. How does this objective apply to you? Here are some ideas.

On the personal side, you will be considering all of humanity, of which you are an important part. Your family also has a special place in the overall scheme of things. The people you work with and your company all are parts of the picture. Without presuming the results of your personal brainstorming efforts, here are some areas you may wish to consider to get started.[1] (Figure 6.2)

If we brainstorm for our whole person, the picture of work, family, and individual and general human interests should all fit into the picture within the context of the objective statement.

At this point, you may wish to go ahead and do your own personal brainstorming, writing down all the areas you would like to improve or change. Once you have a page or two of ideas, continue with the next section.

The List

The list, also known as the checklist, is a powerful tool. To use it to its best advantage, we need some solid rules that develop into work habits. Let's start with the general concept.

Career needs and goals

Emotional needs

Family needs and interests

Financial needs and interests

Health and fitness interests and requirements

Intellectual interests

Need for sense of accomplishments

Social needs and interests

Spiritual needs and interests

Has anything been left out of this list?

FIGURE 6.2 Brainstorming areas

Why have a list in the first place? It's usually because we have too many things to do and it's easy to forget to do something . . . maybe even something important.

By itemizing action items on a list, we have given ourselves a tool to ensure that each item is done. So the first rule is that every necessary action item that is not done immediately is added to the list. By the same token, each action item completed is removed from the list *only when it is absolutely completed.*

The list always exists. If you complete every action item on the list, the blank paper must be available at all times for the next item to be added. Since change is a continuous process, there is always something to add.

Five Whys

This tool is not for everybody, nor for all times, but it's fascinating. Take an idea: I want to learn to play the piano this year.

Ask yourself the question, "Why?" If you're like most folks, you're in trouble already. Although it seems like a simple question, as we said earlier, people are complicated. Our reasons for doing things are not always clear. Let's invent an answer: Because I enjoy music.

Now, ask the question again: "Why?" Once you have taken an inventory of your actual needs and the potential advantages and disadvantages of practicing the piano, you may find that you don't want that after all. A new radio may seem like a better investment than piano lessons.

The first or second "why" can stimulate a lot of good solid thinking and change. If you can get all the way to the fifth "why" without considering the meaning of life, you're not thinking hard enough.

There is no doubt in my mind that the question "why" can change your life. Are you ready to ask it? Why?

Notice that with the use of this tool, we are making a transition from a creative process of generating ideas to an analytical process. Challenge the "why" of each idea on your personal list. Ask all Five Whys if you can. If you can't get to five, do as many as you can for each item on your list.

(Note: Here is a good place to stop and work your personal list.)

Prioritizing and the Decision Matrix

Prioritizing is a useful tool, but it has one pitfall: Prioritizing behavior can never compensate for a lack of capacity. What does this mean? If you have 20 jobs to do today, and you just don't have enough time to do all 20 jobs, and all 20 jobs absolutely must be done, then you need help. Yes, you can prioritize them, but by the end of the day, they all must be completed. Prioritizing will not make that happen. Don't try to use prioritizing to solve this type of problem. Increase capacity, either by becoming more efficient or by getting help.

When not addressed to a capacity problem, prioritizing can be a powerful tool in producing change. Table 6.1 shows examples of criteria by which you can prioritize your personal list.

Not all the criteria listed in the table have solid numbers associated with them. We must invent a way to use them in our prioritizing activity. One simple tool that helps is the matrix. A matrix is nothing more than an organizing of numbers. In this case, we will organize our numbers in a way that will help us make a decision.

CRITERIA	TYPE OF VALUE
Time constraint	Rank order
Expense	Dollar value
Feasibility	Rank order
Impact on issue at hand	Rank order
Forecast benefit	Dollar estimate

TABLE 6.1 Examples of criteria

We will prioritize our brainstorming list according to the key points in the Fuller objective. Table 6.2 shows one way to do it.

You will notice that we have used examples of three rating systems in the table:

1. A 0–1 system for things that can be judged by black-and-white terms. They either are present or not.

2. A 0–1–2–3–4 system for items that could each contribute in varying degrees to our objective. This is a simple example of weighting. You can give extra weight to any item as you see fit.

3. A 0–1–2–3 system for items that have shades of gray. The use of the word "somewhat" helps identify this concept.

Notice that all scales are arranged so that the higher score indicates a more positive response. This arrangement allows the results to reflect the traditional grading system used in most schools where the higher grade is more positive. It also ensures that one scale will not operate in reverse.

Now, let's look at our brainstorming ideas from Figure 2.3 in light of the Fuller objective by constructing an evaluation matrix (Table 6.3).

When we look at the layout of our chart, we see that unequal weights are given to individual points because we used different scales. We may not wish to do this. Some constructive thinking

OBJECTIVE	EVALUATION
Personal—done by me	1 if it is done by me 0 if it isn't
Improve physical protection and support of all human lives	0 if it does nothing 1 for company 2 for personal 3 for family 4 for all human lives Add to produce total
Remove undesirable constraints	0 if it does nothing 1 if it does little 2 if it does something substantial 3 if it does a lot
Improve individual initiatives	0 absolutely not 1 somewhat unproductive 2 somewhat productive 3 very productive
Not doable by organizations	0 if this can be done by organizations 1 if it cannot be done by organizations

TABLE 6.2 Prioritization of brainstorming list

must be done to ensure that the rating scale reflects the actual degree of importance we place on each item. In other words, improving of physical protection can accumulate a total of 10 points, while other scales get only zero or one. If we are going to add across the line to accumulate total points, then improving physical protection will receive about 10 times the weight as some other items, and about three times the weight of others.

The beauty of a rating matrix is that you can set it up to weigh the relative importance of individual items any way you see fit. Assuming that each item in the Fuller objective has equal weight, let's standardize our scores so that each item can have a maximum of 10 points (Table 6.4).

	DONE BY ME	PROTECTION/ SUPPORT	REMOVE CONSTRAINTS	IMPROVE INITIATIVES	NOT DOABLE BY ORGANIZATIONS
Shape	1	5	0	1	1
Piano	1	0	0	1	1
Savings	1	5	1	1	1
Useful	1	N/A	N/A	N/A	1
Habits	1	10	1	1	1

TABLE 6.3 Evaluation matrix

	DONE BY ME	PROTECTION/ SUPPORT	REMOVE CONSTRAINTS	IMPROVE INITIATIVES	NOT DOABLE BY ORGANIZATIONS
Maximum	1	10	3	3	1
Multiply by	10	1	3.3	3.3	10
		New Matrix			
Shape	10	5	0	3.3	10
Piano	10	0	0	3.3	10
Savings	10	5	3.3	3.3	10
Useful	10	N/A	N/A	N/A	10
Habits	10	10	3.3	3.3	10

TABLE 6.4 Standardized evaluation matrix

Before calculating, we notice two ways to simplify our analysis.

First, all suggestions received the same score for two criteria. As a result, these criteria will have no effect on the order of evaluation. If this is really the way we feel, then they can be dropped from the matrix at this time. If our true views are not reflected by these numbers, then the rating should be changed so that our views will be expressed.

In the case of "feeling useful to others," we have discovered that this is a result, rather than a direct action. It will be a likely outcome from accomplishing our objective statement. Yet it may indicate a weakness. In our brainstorming, did we think up any suggestions that would directly contribute to the well-being of others? Since this is actually a missing element, we must either brainstorm to fill the void or eliminate this item from the analysis.

Simplify your own matrix now, to eliminate ideas with the same score for all criteria.

Now, we have the simplest expression of our matrix (Table 6.5).

In Table 6.6, the matrix is rank-ordered by total points.

According to our decision matrix, becoming free of habits is the most valuable issue we could work on because it has the highest total evaluated score. Does this agree with our thoughts? With our feelings? If not, we must go back to identify the problem.

Assuming that this evaluation were perfect, we could work on the first item (becoming free of habits) with the confidence of knowing that we will feel good about the result.

One final problem with our matrix, though, is that no consideration has been given to work-related items, which are important to our personal objectives. While at work, we identified three things we could do to improve the situation there. The results are summarized in Figure 6.3.

We must now put our workplace opportunities and our personal opportunities into the same evaluation so that we can begin with a clear set of priorities which will allow us to act as whole individuals. We must also compare our real numbers, like time and cost, to our comparative rankings, like feasibility and impact. There is no single best way, but here are some ideas.

1. Pick the most important criterion, and use that ranking only. This assumes that the others all put together would never outweigh the single most important consideration. Let's say that the impact on the problem was the most important factor. In that case, we would select the revised form option, because it ranked highest on that criterion.

	PROTECTION/ SUPPORT	REMOVE CONSTRAINTS	IMPROVE INITIATIVES	TOTAL
Shape	5	0	3.3	8.3
Piano	0	0	3.3	3.3
Savings	5	3.3	3.3	11.6
Habits	10	3.3	3.3	16.6

TABLE 6.5 Simplified matrix

	PROTECTION/ SUPPORT	REMOVE CONSTRAINTS	IMPROVE INITIATIVES	TOTAL
Habits	10	3.3	3.3	16.6
Savings	5	3.3	3.3	11.6
Shape	5	0	3.3	8.3
Piano	0	0	3.3	3.3

TABLE 6.6 Rank-ordered matrix

2. Use some factors as disqualifiers. Take cost as an example. Perhaps one item, like skills training, is prohibitively expensive at this time. You can weed it out on that basis. The other two options are less far apart and cost may no longer be a consideration.

3. Consolidate two criteria. Here we have time and money. We could translate the time into its corresponding monetary value for the people involved and make it all one cost column.

There are many other ways to deal with the decision. The most important concept is that we want to use a realistic, factual basis for establishing our priorities. If we do this on a regular basis, we will get much better value out of each decision. Since our criteria

ACTION ITEM	TIME	COST	FEASIBILITY	IMPACT
Communication skills	10 hours	$5,000	2	1
Toolbox meeting	1 hour	$200	1	2
Revised form	5 hours	$100	3	3

FIGURE 6.3 Matrix evaluation

	PROTECTION/ SUPPORT	REMOVE CONSTRAINTS	IMPROVE INITIATIVES	TOTAL
Habits	10	3.3	3.3	16.6
Savings	5	3.3	3.3	11.6
Shape	5	0	3.3	8.3
Piano	0	0	3.3	3.3
Communication	5	5	5	15
Revised form	0	5	9	14
Toolbox meeting	0	4	10	14

TABLE 6.7 Personal and work-related matrix

are broader in our personal matrix, we will evaluate our work-related ideas using the new criteria (Table 6.7).

On this pass, we again notice that we have a criterion which fails to differentiate one idea from another, so we will remove it from the list. We also have more flexibility because everything is on a 10-point scale. Table 6.8 shows both personal and work activities rated on the same scale.

What we have produced is a rank ordering of doable activities that will meet our personal requirements. According to our analysis, the most valuable activity is to become free of habits. This is a personal activity that will also apply to our work environment.

	PROTECTION/ SUPPORT	REMOVE CONSTRAINTS	IMPROVE INITIATIVES	TOTAL
Habits	10	3.3	3.3	16.6
Communication	10	10	5	15.0
Revised	0	5	9	14.0
Toolbox	0	4	10	14.0
Savings	5	3.3	3.3	11.6
Shape	5	0	3.3	8.3
Piano	0	0	3.3	3.3

TABLE 6.8 Final evaluation matrix

The second item, improving our communication skills, came into our plan as a work-related item, but it is hard to deny that it will have a positive personal effect, too.

We have identified the vital few. Let's keep the entire list, though, and treat it as a long-term agenda. We'll put it in our tickle file for six months from now, and look at it again to see if the situation has changed.

Visualization

This technique is widely known for its success with professional athletes. For our purposes, we want to use our imagination to create a detailed image of what it will look like when we accomplish our goal. You will need quiet time to use this technique. Taking our top two items, becoming free of habits and improving our personal communications, we might visualize these images:

1. Being free of habits (coffee and cookies)

   Walking past the vending machine
   Deep satisfaction of avoiding the cookies
   Feeling physically better—strong and well-rested

2. Improving personal communications

Friends welcoming me warmly

Continuous stream of lunch invitations

Warm feelings in exchanging compliments

Fewer arguments

Sense of satisfaction in getting things done

These are just a few images you might conjure up. How strong an image can you create? Consider all five senses as well as internal feelings. (Note: Now would be a good time to visualize the top priority item in your personal list.)

Flowchart

The flowchart has been in use for years in systems design, process control, computer programming, and other fields. It's not surprising to see it used also in quality improvement.

The flowchart is used to describe the order of events in a process. In addition, it can be used to:

- Help identify the individual steps in a process.
- Compare an actual process to an original design.
- Communicate changes and increase awareness.

You can buy templates with scores of symbols on them to show all sorts of detail, but to create a good flowchart, you only need a few symbols:[2]

- A rectangle to represent a task.
- A diamond to represent a decision.
- A line to connect two symbols.
- An arrowhead to show the direction of flow or action.

Anything else, though sometimes useful, can actually interfere with the ability of other people to understand your chart. A flowchart starts at the top of the page, and goes to the bottom of the page. If you need more than one page, put a note at the bottom that says "go to next page."

From the individual user's point of view, systems frequently start out looking like the one shown in Figure 6.4. I call this the

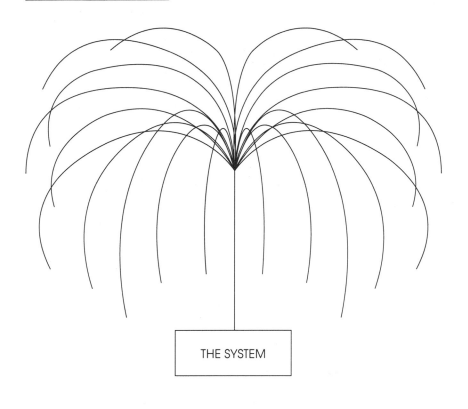

THE SYSTEM

FIGURE 6.4 Phillips Phlowchart

Phillips Phlowchart, in honor of Richard W. Phillips, who originally drew it. It is the best example I have seen to express how confusing a large system can be to the typical user. Even a well-organized system can appear to the user as an endless maze of paths leading nowhere.[3]

A process should be as simple as possible. The more complicated a process is, the more steps it has, and the more decisions involved, the more opportunity there is to introduce error into the system. Error is undesirable because the system is not required to produce error. If error does not meet your requirements, then why build in more opportunities for error?

A good system is the simplest possible system for a given purpose. A system that isn't understood can't be managed. Once you have defined your system the way it is, you may wish to consider how it can be simplified, for example, by drawing your flowchart up-and-down more than sideways (fewer branches make the system simpler), by having more boxes than diamonds (the fewer decisions required, the simpler the system), and by making each box better defined (the clearer the instructions, the easier to follow them). There should also be as few ways to get to an individual step as possible. Figure 6.5 shows an example of a simple flowchart.

Why is all this so important? Because the larger and more complicated a system gets, the harder it is to keep track of it. You don't have to look far to find a system that has gotten large and cumbersome, but doesn't accomplish its original objective. In government, for example, there are many expansive and expensive programs that provide little service for the cost; in business, many companies have elaborate computerized inventory control systems, yet still experience poor service from inventory; in education, we appear to be suffering from a permanent deterioration in delivery of education to the student at continually increasing cost. These systems are typically built up (sometimes called ad hoc) from smaller systems, without considering the system as a whole. The modifications seemed to be a good idea at the time, but the result can be messy.

You can see that even the flowchart shown in Figure 6.5 is more complicated than it needs to be. Even a simple process can be improved. This time, let's go through the flowchart from bottom to top, keeping in mind the expected result: to be on time all the time. (Figure 6.6)

As you can see from looking at the flowchart, none of the paths will result in 100 percent on-time performance, so a new solution must be found, preferably a simpler one. Where I work, there is an alternate route with no train tracks, but it takes about five minutes longer. Now, look at the flowchart if we take this alternate route.

Try diagramming a flowchart of one of your own procedures. You may be amazed at the number of decisions and actions taken in even a simple process. As we did in the example, do a second pass from bottom to top. You may find that something has been left out, or that you must consider other actions to get your desired

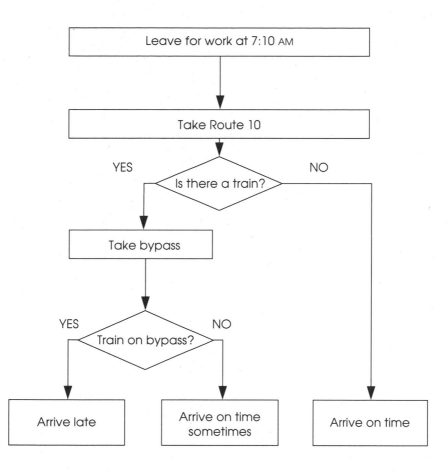

FIGURE 6.5 Simple flowchart

result. When you are finished, you should find that each step produces all the requirements needed to go on to the next step. Now that you have defined the system as it is, you can consider how it can be simplified or improved.

You may have to revise the flowchart many times before you are satisfied with the result, which is fine. A flowchart is a working document. Things change, and when they do, you can use the flowchart to consider how to change your process to adapt to the new conditions.

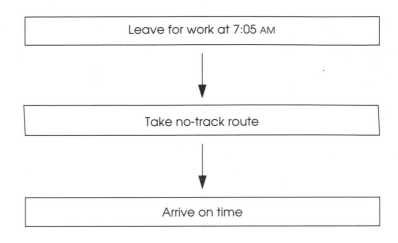

FIGURE 6.6 Simplified flowchart

Frequently, the act of constructing a flowchart can help reveal the reasons why something isn't working, especially when you show on the same page the actual person who is supposed to do each step and exactly what he or she is supposed to do. Figure 6.7 shows an example of a form which has worked for me. Observe that by adding specific information about each step, the value of a flowchart as a communication tool is enhanced.

The Objective Statement

My objective in this section is to describe the objective statement, explain its purpose, define its elements, and provide guidelines for its use. The preceding sentence is an objective statement. Each different organization has its own set of requirements, but good objective statements have much in common.

The purpose of an objective statement is to clearly define the who, what, when, where, and how of a particular action or program. The objective statement is both a thinking tool and a communication tool. It is a thinking tool because the process of creating an objective statement forces us to think through exactly what it is we want to do. It is a communication tool because, if it is clearly written, it will describe to others what it is we are trying to accomplish and how we will know when it's been done.

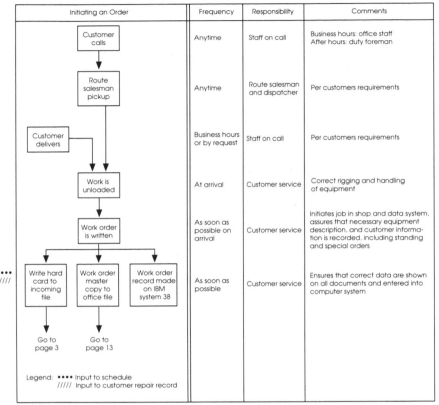

FIGURE 6.7 Enhanced flowchart

An objective statement has three parts of speech: a noun, a verb, and an object. The noun can be "I" or "we." If it is anything else, it does not express a commitment. The verb should be an action verb. After all, we want to take action, don't we? The object should clearly show the thing(s) on which you want to act. Finally, while not a figure of speech, we need an indicator. Without that, we cannot measure our success. Another way to look at an objective statement is to say that we want the who, what, when, where, and how of our proposed actions. Here's a summary:

Who:	I or we
What:	object
When:	should start now, indicator shows finish
Where:	will be included if needed
How:	may be implicit, but should be stated if the method is not obvious

When all of these items are included, are clear and understandable, and all fit together, you've got an objective statement.

Now, let's go back to our original statement and see how we did: My objective in this section is to describe the objective statement, explain its purpose, define its elements, and provide guidelines for its use.

Who:	"Our objective" may be more appropriate in an organization, but it also takes away some of the power.
What:	Here we have three points: 1. To explain the purpose 2. To define the elements 3. To provide guidelines for use
When:	"Now" is implicit, because I am writing a book. In other cases, it may need to be stated.
Where:	Again, in this instance, the place is clearly right here.
How:	It is clear the "how" is by writing this section.
Indicator:	We have three indicators in the "what" section.

Now, let's evaluate our performance against our original objectives:

1. Did we explain the purpose? Yes.
2. Did we define the elements? Yes.
3. Did we provide guidelines? No.

We can see from our review that we have not yet established guidelines for use of the objective statement, so here they are:

Be as thorough as possible in stating your objective.

Be clear in the way you state it.

Be sure that it makes sense, and is consistent with your goals.

Finally, once you are satisfied with your objective statement, *make it happen.*

(Note: Now would be a good time to consider an objective statement and flowchart of your own top item.)

GRAPHIC TOOLS

Graphic tools have a special place in the world of quality improvement for two key reasons: They can provide a clear impression or summary of analytical results, and they facilitate communication of these results. Let's look at a typical real life example.

At Acme Widgets, the cost of expense items used in the shop seems to have increased greatly over the past year. These items include paint brushes, flashlight batteries, and a wide variety of relatively low-cost items. Seizing this fabulous opportunity for a quality improvement project, the manager calls a team together to begin work. The computer reports the financial results on a monthly basis. These are good data, but it is quickly discovered that the data do not reflect the actions that have caused the increased expense. These data must be converted to relevant information.

Since all the programmers are busy on other projects, the team decides to reorganize these costs on a spreadsheet, compiled manually, which presents only the information they want to see. Based on detailed analysis, the team recommended that the shop foremen be brought together to make them aware of the increase and to suggest how it might be controlled. The spreadsheet showed clearly that the meeting produced results in May (Figure 6.8).

Tables of data, while useful, do not necessarily draw attention to the important facts. A general awareness of the degree of improvement did not occur until the results were presented in graphic

	MAR	APR	MAY	JUN	JUL
Group A	$2,723	$3,268	$425	$5,339	$10,084
Group B	2,108	4,161	(475)	2,374	2,774
Group C	3,333	2,192	861	1,434	1,940
Group D	(254)	376	(24)	(117)	195
Total	15,965	20,121	11,828	17,291	24,729
Recap*	8,056	10,123	11,045	8,623	9,735
Percent Recap	50%	50%	93%	51%	39%

*Represents amount recaptured through special cost-saving activities

FIGURE 6.8 Expense spreadsheet

form. Look at Figure 6.9 and see the ease with which you can observe the results. Graphic presentation focuses the attention on key results. Imagine the difference in impact a graphic presentation might have on someone who is not already familiar with your area of inquiry.

This simple example should give an idea of the power of graphic presentation. The growth of personal computer-based graphic and presentation software over the past few years is evidence that the power of graphics is gaining recognition.

Charts and Graphs

Charts and graphs have certain common features that will aid in presenting information. For instance, each chart or graph should be clearly labeled at the top. Why the top? Because people read from top to bottom, and this label will prepare them for the information they are about to receive. Mental preparation will facilitate understanding.

All lines, bars, or segments should be clearly labeled. Again, if the person who is seeing the chart doesn't know what they are looking at, the information will be missing even though the data are presented.

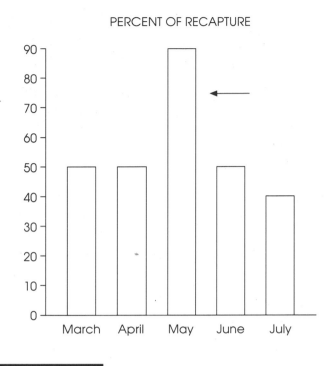

FIGURE 6.9 Spreadsheet results converted to bar chart

The source of the data should be presented. I like to take the extra step of keeping the source data stapled to the back of the chart or graph, so I don't have to go back to research the data every time I have a question. The scale of the data should also be clearly defined.

Keep it simple. There is sometimes a tendency to put too much information on one chart. Say only one thing per chart. If you are trying to say two things, use two charts.

Bar Chart

Figure 6.9 shows a bar chart. The purpose of a bar chart is to show comparative data. For instance, if you want to track your progress on your five key goals, you might select a bar chart. Along the horizontal (x) axis are the categories. The vertical (y) axis is used for quantity. In the next example, percentage of completion is the indicator.

In the area of communication, anything that helps others understand your point should be used. Although a bar chart can be turned around so that the x axis shows quantity, most readers are used to seeing quantity on the y axis. Since this style of presentation will make it easier for others to understand, it should be used.

Histograms

A histogram is used to show degree of dispersion of items in a population. For example, we may wish to compare scores on a competitive examination. We select a histogram to show the dispersion of these scores.

Like the bar chart, the category (or in this case, range) is presented along the horizontal axis. The frequency of occurrence is presented along the vertical axis. All the labeling constraints mentioned above apply to histograms as well.

Figure 6.10 shows a histogram. A histogram shows frequency of occurrence, while a bar chart shows quantity.

Pie Charts

A pie chart is an excellent way to show relative proportion or percentage among various categories contained in a whole area. For example, how many people in your work group are college graduates, junior college graduates, and high school graduates.

The power of the pie chart is that it clearly shows the relationship of one to the other while at the same time shows the relationship of each to the whole.

Florida Power and Light has a highly structured way to present this chart, which they have allowed me to pass along in Figure 6.11.[4]

Theory of Lines

Theory of Lines,[5] or Queueing Theory, was first explained to me by Dr. Tom Johnson of the University of South Florida, an inveterate golfer and outstanding human being. I have always preferred the name Theory of Lines because it is more commonly understood.

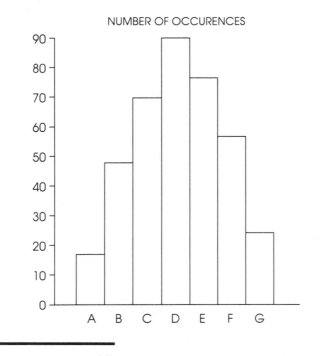

FIGURE 6.10 Histogram

The concept is simple. We wait in line all the time, even some-times when we don't realize it. Lines can be managed if we know how fast the inputs come in and how long it takes to handle one. The Disney organization is renowned for its management of lines. In fact, it is hard to imagine how they could handle as many people as they do without a detailed understanding of lines and how they work. But the theory applies to things as well as people, and to a variety of situations, for instance:

- Customer service desk: How many people are re-quired to service a certain number of customers?

- Telephone switching: How many lines are needed to handle incoming calls?

- Machine shop: How many workstations (man/ma-chine combinations) are required to handle the flow of work?

All of these situations, and many more, can be analyzed with

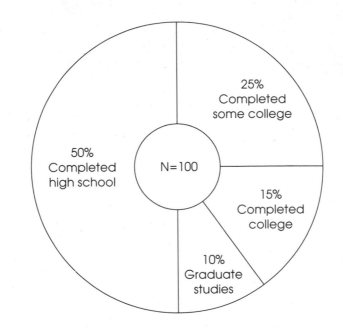

FIGURE 6.11 Pie chart of educational levels in sample work group

line theory and monitored to ensure rates of service that will keep your customers satisfied.

Stated simply, the length of the line depends on two things: how fast units are coming in and how fast they are processed. Also, the average waiting time can be calculated using the same numbers. Here are the mathematics:

l = arrival rate
m = service rate

p = service intensity = $\dfrac{l}{m}$

L = length of line = $\dfrac{l}{m-l}$

W = average time in line = $\dfrac{p}{m-l}$

Although there is much more to this theory, you can obtain a wealth of practical information based on how fast items are coming in and how fast they are processed.

Usually, you are not in control of the inputs (how many customer calls you have in an hour), but you can control how fast you handle them, either by increasing the speed of handling or by adding more service providers. Let's take an example and work it through, using some of the ideas we have accumulated along the way.

Freddy's Machine Shop rebuilds clutches. Because that's all they do, they have figured out that it takes an average of three hours to disassemble, clean, pick parts, repair, and reassemble a typical clutch. Freddy has six full-time clutch mechanics, and a backlog of 200 jobs waiting to be repaired. Freddy's rough guess of his flow of business is as follows.

l = new jobs per day	20
m = jobs completed per day	16
length of line	200

Based on these numbers, we can see that Freddy is in big trouble. Because he can't handle as many jobs as he has coming in, his backlog is growing by four jobs each day. No wonder he feels overwhelmed.

In order to put this in a frame of reference, let's look at a progression from least complicated to most complicated by looking at Freddy's situation. Having become aware of a problem, and having gone through his five stages of personal change, he will be going through the following problem-solving steps:

1. Problem identification: begin collecting data
2. Problem analysis: analyzing basic data using charts and graphs
   Scaling the data: making graphics fit the data
   Averaging: looking for central tendency
3. Planning
4. Data collection: gathering more specific data called for by the analysis above
5. Data interpretation: using graphic and other tools to understand what the numbers reveal

6. Action: establishing controls or changes based on analysis; achieving control by continuous comparison

7. Appraisal: evaluation of project; improving control if results indicate additional opportunity

For now, we will focus on the application of Theory of Lines, but remember that Freddy must be aware of all seven steps to gain the most from the process. Since Freddy is a quality improvement enthusiast, he is anxious to apply quality techniques in his workplace.

At first, Freddy had no idea how many clutches he repaired each day, although he thought he did. In order to get a better handle on the subject, Freddy began a run chart. A run chart is usually a good place to start when looking at a process for the first time. A run chart simply shows performance over time. In this chart, he shows the number of jobs he completes each day. Figure 6.12 is his first chart.

Freddy always wondered why he was tired on Friday afternoon. By charting his work, he began to realize that each Friday, he worked extra hard to catch up with his pile of incoming jobs. Just the act of charting his work has already helped Freddy to understand the situation better. Now, he's ready to take another step.

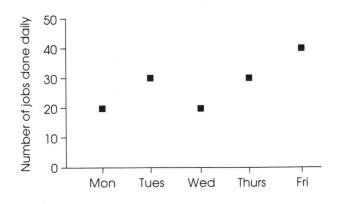

FIGURE 6.12 Run Chart

In this case, Freddy had the right scale because his daily counts did not run off the top or the bottom of the chart. Sometimes, we're not so lucky and we have to change the chart to allow for more or less of a range of scores. In Freddy's case, he couldn't go less than zero, so half the problem was solved automatically.

There are two things we should watch: the average and the range (distance from highest to lowest). We can see the entire range because we were lucky enough to pick the right scale for our graph. There are several ways to take an average.

- The mean is the arithmetic average (the total divided by the number of items):
- The median is the center-most score. If you arrange the numbers from high to low, then the one in the middle is the median.
- The mode is the most frequently occurring score. This is used in cases where one score may be repeated many times.

Each has its strengths and weaknesses. For now, we'll stick with the arithmetic average, or mean. Freddy adds the number of jobs completed in a day, then divides by the number of days to get his average.

20	day 1
30	day 2
20	day 3
30	day 4
40	day 5
140	divided by 5 = 28 jobs per day

Originally, Freddy thought the average was 16. This serves to illustrate a point about managing by fact. In the practical world, we frequently make assumptions about the way things are, based on a variety of inputs. Nearly as frequently, we find that when we focus on an issue and measure it, the facts are not as we had thought. Freddy found that he was seriously mistaken, and now he knows it.

Shorthand for mean is an x with a bar over it ($\overline{X}$). It is called "x bar." You will often find this on charts instead of the word

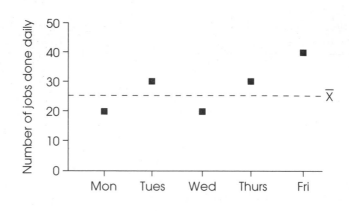

FIGURE 6.13 Run chart with mean

"mean." Now, let's look at the chart Freddy has produced in Figure 6.13. Observe that by adding the mean to the run chart it is easy to see if you are above or below the average.

Freddy can now see the variation in his work, but the pile is still growing. So he must find out how many jobs are coming *in* per day. In the meantime, however, he has figured out that, with certain improvements, he could perform 28 jobs each day, and not be so tired on Friday. So he made a little challenge to himself that he will never do less than 28 jobs per day on Monday through Thursday. On Friday, he would do only the jobs needed to total 140 for the week. And if he finishes on time, he will go to the movies. In other words, Freddy will standardize his performance at a rate that will achieve the desired result. He will have to organize himself around this concept, and measure his results on a daily basis if he wants to avoid a catastrophe each Friday. He will then reward himself when he accomplishes his weekly goal.

There is still the matter of the pile of incoming work. Freddy finds that the new average is 30 jobs each day. This means that the pile grows, on the average, by two pieces each day, even with his improvements. This explains why he's running out of room in the shop. Now, Freddy has a new target. He must average 30 jobs per day to keep up with incoming work and keep his customers from being unhappy because it takes so long to get their work back. He counts the clutches in the pile, and finds that (even with the extra work) it contains 120 pieces, or about three days' work. So, Freddy goes back to the drawing board and comes up with the run chart shown in Figure 6.14.

As you can see, Freddy increased his target to 30 and continues to work on Saturday to get caught up. At his new rate and with the additional day, he will eliminate the pile in three weeks. Because he has a chart to track his performance, Freddy will now know his situation from day to day. All he has to do is track the number of jobs completed and look at the incoming pile. Once he has achieved this steady state, he can compute the customers' waiting times. Using our input rate, service rate, and the line theory formulas, we can see the change from the customer's point of view when we increase processing rate. Here is the original estimated situation:

$$l\ = \text{arrival rate} \qquad\qquad\qquad 20$$
$$m = \text{service rate} \qquad\qquad\qquad 30$$

$$p\ = \text{service intensity} = \frac{l}{m} \qquad\qquad .67$$

$$L = \text{length of line} = \frac{l}{m-l} \qquad\qquad 2$$

$$W = \text{average time in line} = \frac{p}{m-l} \qquad .07$$

In plain words, the length of line should have been two pieces, and the average time in line of a job is .07 days, or less than one hour. But Freddy was way off on his estimate of incoming jobs.

The improvement in Freddy's performance gave him a competitive advantage. Now he is getting 30 jobs in per day. Let's look at the effects of managing his capacity to control his customer service. He has increased his service rate to give himself some breathing room:

$$l\ = \text{arrival rate} \qquad\qquad\qquad 30$$
$$m = \text{service rate} \qquad\qquad\qquad 32$$

$$p = \text{service intensity} = \frac{l}{m} \qquad\qquad .94$$

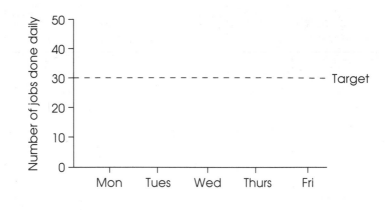

FIGURE 6.14 Run chart with target

$$L = \text{length of line} = \frac{l}{m-l} \qquad 15$$

$$W = \text{average time in line} = \frac{p}{m-l} \qquad .47$$

If he increases his capacity by 10 percent, from 31 to 34, he can cut the customer's waiting time by almost 80 percent. For each subsequent 10 percent improvement, the benefit diminishes. Using Theory of Lines, it is possible to find the best balance between additional capacity (a cost) and quality service to customers (with the additional revenue).

Figure 6.15 shows how the key indicators are affected by increases in capacity. The benefits diminish as additional improvements are made. Figure 6.16 shows how half the total possible line reduction is achieved by adding only one additional clutch service per day.

After one month, Freddy has seen two movies and worked three Saturdays, but he hasn't eliminated the incoming work pile. It seems that his customers were so pleased with how fast he got their clutches back to them that they told their friends. Now, he has to plan for another expansion. He will have to monitor the incoming work on a regular basis. This is the beginning of process control. (Beyond this simple example is a world of more detailed statistics.

INPUT	OUTPUT	SERVICE INTENSITY	LINE LENGTH	WAIT
30	31	.97	30	.97
30	32	.94	15	.47
30	33	.91	10	.30
30	34	.88	7.5	.22
30	35	.86	6	.17
30	36	.83	5	.14
30	37	.81	4	.12
30	38	.79	3.75	.10
30	39	.77	3.33	.09
30	40	.75	3	.08
30	50	.60	1.5	.03
30	60	.50	1	.02

FIGURE 6.15 Key line indicators (assuming inputs of 30 pieces per day)

When you are ready for more, Chapters 3 and 4 of Juran and Gryna's *Quality Planning and Analysis* would be a good place to start.)[6]

On a personal level, we each have things that must be done. They come at a varying rate and take varying amounts of time and energy to complete. Yet we can use the same principle of line theory to manage our work. Here's a simple example.

At one stage in the process of writing this book, I had a revision deadline for ASQC Quality Press. In order to accomplish that objective, I had to complete one chapter per week for a period of 12 weeks. I used a checklist to keep track of my progress and was able to ensure that this task was done. I was treating this project as a line with an original length of 12 and a rate of service of one per week, with no new incoming priorities. If this worked (which it did), then I could apply the same technique to all my incoming tasks and manage my capacity accordingly. I may not need a

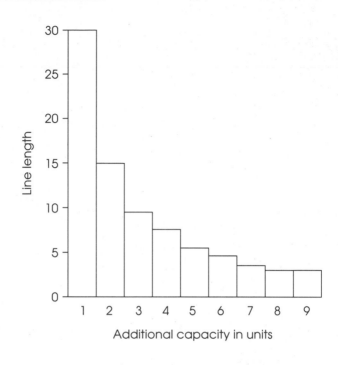

FIGURE 6.16 Graphic expression of Figure 6.15

calculator to determine when more is coming in than is going back out (I did put in some extra hours), but the same principle applies. Any line can be managed. The tools are available and the concept is simple. You have to get it out the door at least as fast as it comes in or you'll fall behind, usually with negative consequences. Better organization in managing this function can provide many improvement opportunities in our personal and professional lives.

Cause-and-Effect Diagram

Sometimes, you know what needs to be corrected, but you are not sure why it is out of kilter. The idea is to find the root cause and address the "disease" rather than the "symptoms." One tool to help you do this is the cause-and-effect diagram, also known as the fishbone diagram, or the Ishikawa diagram (after its inventor). The fishbone diagram shows the end result (or problem) in the box at the right side. The fishbones are all the contributing factors.

It helps to break the contributing causes into general areas to really understand a problem. One way to divide causes uses man (or woman), method, machine, materials, measurement, and information. Using this method, the "fish" would have five large bones, with individual little bones attached to each one. Figure 6.17 shows the same fishbone diagram divided in that way.

Frequently in office situations, materials are not an issue. To analyze possible causes in office situations using people, procedures, and information may work better. Even in the shop, machines and materials are controlled by these three elements.

1. *People* make mistakes. Don't be surprised if many of the errors you discover are "human error." Based on experience, you may as well put training and motivation on the people fishbone, because you will probably find the need for both eventually.

2. In order to so something consistently, you must want to do it right, you must have a *procedure* consistently applied, and you must have all the *information* necessary to carry out that procedure.

3. At the same time, you may wish to add *standards* to the procedure fishbone.

Figure 6.18 shows the same chart, redrawn. Use either method or one of your own invention. The important thing about this method is to use the fishbone to organize ideas about the causes for your problem area, then organize them in a way which will draw attention to the interrelations of these causes. Understanding relationships has become so important that seven new quality tools have been developed to deal with these issues.[7]

Since the purpose of the fishbone diagram is to break a problem into its root causes, you should not feel restricted in how to lay it out. The process of constructing a fishbone diagram will lead to a detailed examination of the situation. It is therefore the thoughtful analysis that is important, rather than the actual shape of the fish.

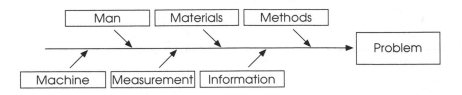

FIGURE 6.17 Basic fishbone diagram

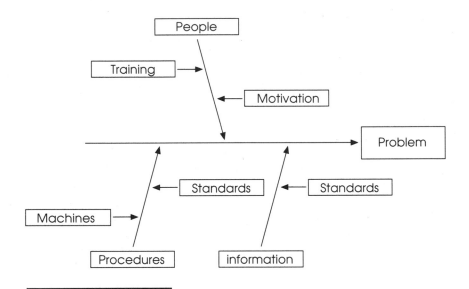

FIGURE 6.18 Alternate fishbone

Pareto Analysis

Vilfredo Pareto was an economist and social philosopher who lived around the turn of the century in Italy.[8] He is remembered for his observation that the distribution of total wealth was uneven. When he charted amount of wealth by percentage of the population, he came up with a graph very much like Figure 6.19. The top few percent controlled the majority of the total wealth, with decreasing wealth down through the brackets. Juran and others found that this type of distribution occurs frequently and in

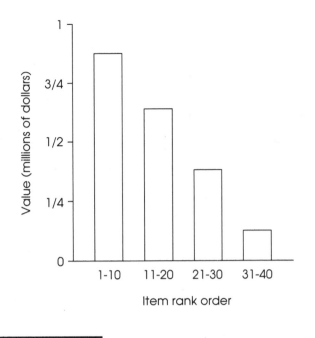

FIGURE 6.19 Pareto distribution of inventory investment

many places. Since that time, Pareto's law has been popularized as the 80/20 rule: 80 percent of the distribution comes from 20 percent of the elements.

Figure 6.19 shows an example of inventory investment organized by dollars per item.

In the figure, 80 percent of the investment is in 20 percent of the parts. This distribution can occur in customer sales (80 percent of the sales come from 20 percent of the customers), human relations (80 percent of the suggestions come from 20 percent of the employees), or other areas. But it may just as well not apply. In gathering your data, you will want to be objective in determining if your facts support a Pareto distribution. Let's take a look at a different example. This time we are looking at sales by customer. First, we'll construct a bar chart, shown in Figure 6.20.

As you can see, there is a wide variation of sales by customer. Although organized by customer, this chart does not give us all the information available. Let's reorganize our bars in decreasing order.

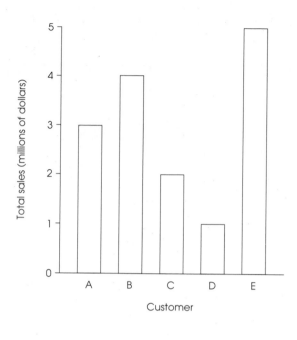

FIGURE 6.20 Pareto chart of sales by customer

By reorganizing our chart in descending order, we can see the effect of Pareto's law. If we grouped our customers in groups of two, three or four, the distribution would be about the same. Figure 6.21 shows the same distribution as Figure 6.20 reorganized by dollar volume of sales.

Finally, there are a few refinements that you may wish to add because they can help communicate your findings to others. Although they may be interested, they may not have looked at this information in the same depth you have. When cumulative totals are added, as in Figure 6.22, it is easier for others to see the full impact of the so-called Pareto effect.

Pareto charts can be very helpful, as long as we do not stray from the overall objective. For example, if the objective is to serve *all* customers, we may wish to be careful about the actions we take based on Pareto analysis. This technique will show us where most

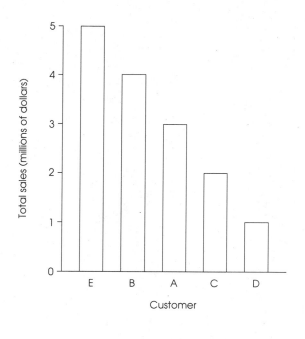

FIGURE 6.21 Bar chart organized by customer

of the customers or dollars or action items are, but it does not imply priority. You may wish to take different actions with different classes of customer, while considering all customers in your overall activities.

One last point deserves mention here: Not every distribution is a normal distribution or a Pareto distribution. In a different company, sales by customer may be arranged in a different way. As mentioned before, use these tools only where they apply. The factual data will tell you that.

Let's switch back to the personal side. It is possible that 80 percent of your personal activities produce only 20 percent of your satisfaction? Let's look at our five original items.

1. Get in shape
2. Learn to play the piano

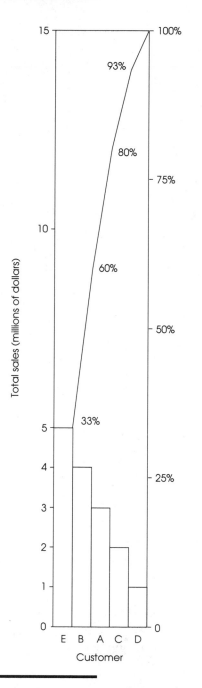

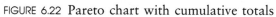

FIGURE 6.22 Pareto chart with cumulative totals

3. Start a savings plan

4. Feel useful to others

5. Be free of habits

If you were to make a checklist and put a mark beside each item every time you thought about it, you might come up with a Pareto-like distribution. It would certainly point the direction to the area which is most frequently on your mind. It is also possible that you could get a greater result in terms of personal satisfaction if you select and focus in on the item which is most on your mind.

Try this with your personal list. If it is useful, keep it. If not, use the other tools.

Statistics

There is more than one way to skin a cat; there is also more than one way to achieve quality improvement. Statistical quality control has a major place in the world of quality improvement. In fact, the very term quality control implies the use of statistics. We would like to approach the subject of statistics with certain key points in mind:

- When approaching an issue, evaluate the merits of both statistical and nonstatistical tools.
- When considering the use of statistics, first check the limits of the particular tool you have in mind (for example, type of distribution or number of individuals in the population or sample) to ensure that your result will be valid.

This information can be found in a good statistics text, which should be at hand if you are going to use statistics on a regular basis. Keeping those two points in mind, let's move on to statistics, starting with its definition as the science of numerical facts, a statement or collection of such facts.

The term "statistics" strikes fear into the heart of the bravest soul. It should. The field of statistics is so dynamic that it is almost impossible to learn all the facets and keep up with new developments. Fortunately, you can achieve a big improvement in your daily operations with just a few basic statistical tools. But be careful. Being able to point out the lobes of the brain does not make one a brain surgeon. This book is not a statistics book. Armed with the general knowledge provided here, you will be able to begin your own education on statistics and perhaps apply some of the most simple, yet powerful statistical tools. Since all aspects of statistics have to do with uncertainty and probability, let's begin with some history of probability.

Histograms and Control Charts

The first statistical tool we will introduce is the histogram. A gentleman by the name of Carl Frederick Gauss[9] showed brilliance in mathematics while still quite young. One of his contributions was in the area of astronomy. In the measurement of the distance to a particular star, repeated observations did not yield the same values. Rather, a series of values which tended to group about a central value was obtained. The histogram is a graphic way to show these values, and his must have looked something like the bell-shape example in Figure 6.10.

The vertical bars represent the frequency with which certain results were obtained. Note that the taller bars are toward the middle of the distribution and that as you move away from the middle, the bars get shorter and eventually disappear. The bars are records of the actual measurements and the curve is a theoretical representation of what all possible measurements might look like. The actual measurements and the curve hardly ever exactly coincide.

Gauss and others found that many measurable items in nature tend to generate a distribution like the one shown in Figure 6.10. Somewhere along the way this distribution took on the name "normal." Control charts for measurements use the properties of the normal distribution in helping to determine the degree of control you have over a process. Properties of the normal distribution can also help estimate how well you are meeting specifications imposed by your customers. A slight digression will serve to help us understand more about how control charts work.

All things vary; nothing remains exactly constant for any period of time. For instance, if you were to sign your name several times, and then if I were to try to copy your signature, you or anyone else could readily tell that it was a forgery. There would be enough difference to see. Although no two of your signatures would be exactly the same, we accept this amount of variation as being "normal." The variation introduced by the forgery, however, is more than we will accept as being normal.

A properly constructed and interpreted control chart allows you to do the same thing with any process. It establishes the acceptable "signature" for the process and indicates whether we are seeing this signature or, instead, something unusual. When we have only the normal variation of the signature, we leave the process alone— any adjustments will simply increase the variation. If we see "abnormal" variation, we investigate to find what is causing it, and make adjustments accordingly. Let's tie the concept of variation, histograms, normal distribution, and control charts together.

Control charts for measurements have a center line, an upper line, and a lower line. The placement of these lines is not arbitrary. The placement of the center line depends on the desired target for the measurement being made. The placement of the upper and lower lines depends on the variability (signature) inherent in the process.

There are two types of information we are interested in: variables and attributes. Variables are things that can be measured or a value placed on, such as length, weight, or thickness. Attributes are things that can be counted or classified as good or bad, pass or fail, number of defects on an assembly, or the number of defectives in a lot or shipment. Variables and attributes require different charts.

Variables

A control chart for variables consists of two sections: one for the average of the process (X-bar chart) and the other is for the range (variability) of the process (R chart).

For example, let's consider Wendy's Washers. Wendy's Washers makes a steel spacer washer. Their customer wants the thickness to be between 150 and 200 mils, with an expected average of 175 mils. Knowing that the measurement process starts with customer requirements, Wendy studied her process and found that the average thickness is 170 and the total variability is somewhat

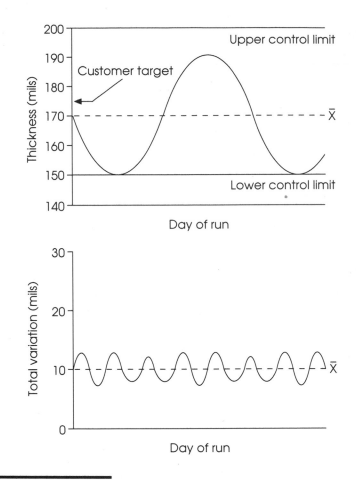

FIGURE 6.23 Basic control chart for a variable

greater than ±21 mils. The histogram in Figure 6.23 shows that Wendy is bumping against the lower specification limit (170 − 21 = 149) and has some space between the process and the upper limit. The $\overline{X}$ chart and range chart show that the average is 170 and the process is in control at this level. The process is under control when all measurements fall within the control limits.[10]

Beginning control limits are set at ±3 sigma to strike the best balance between the two types of potential statistical error.

If Wendy continues to control her process at the present set of conditions, she will always be shipping a small amount (about three pieces per thousand) too small. If Wendy can center at 175 mils instead of 170 and control the process as she has in the past, she will be better off, leaving space between her actual process and both upper and lower control limits.

Just like Wendy, your first step is to learn how to make your process hit average at the correct place. You can then concentrate on reducing variability (narrowing the control limits). In cases where there is a need for a tighter control than you presently have, you must actually decrease variability in addition to centering the process on the target.

There is much information to be derived from the histogram, the control chart, and the accompanying table of statistics. There is also good news for the beginner. There are now computer programs that will compute your statistics and draw your control charts for you. All you have to do is enter the data.

Attributes

Attribute data require only the chart for the average level; they do not require a chart for variability. The reason for this is that with attributes, the average and the variability are linked together. In fact, they are one. For example, when we measure the number of burrs in a run of machine work, we are not grading the burr. It is either present or absent, but has no degree of variability in our measurement. Because attributes are things like number of defectives or percent of impurities, they generally are one-sided distributions. Since you can have no fewer than zero defects, there is only one control limit. Any distribution which is approaching an absolute maximum or minimum will have a one-sided distribution. The result of this situation is that the normal curve (or bell curve) is pushed over to one side (or skewed) providing a somewhat different picture than a normal curve. In these cases there is only one control limit.[11]

Let's consider Stamping Associates. Their customers have told them that no more than 1 percent of the product can have burrs. Figure 6.24 shows the results of Stamping Associates' review. They gathered 100 items per sample and examined each for burrs. They then recorded the number of items per sample that had burrs. The histogram is not as symmetrical as the ones for the last example (variables).

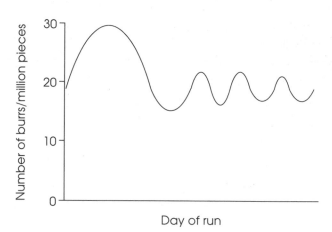

FIGURE 6.24 Control chart for attributes

In each of the above examples, it was assumed that the specifications were reflections of what the customer really needs. Specifications should be set as a joint effort between the customer and supplier. Designed experiments should be run to help determine appropriate specifications. If you find that you are having trouble meeting specifications, the first order of business is to determine if the specifications are really what the customer needs.

Some of the more sophisticated customers are asking for information which ties your process average and variability together with the specifications. When the process is in a good state of control, they take the specification width and divide that by the total statistical width of your process (± 3 sigma). This is call Cp. They also make an adjustment if you are not centering your process at the mid value of their specifications. This is called Cpk. The larger these values are, the better. Some customers are asking for a value of at least 1.33. This value ensures that you are taking up approximately no more than 3/4 of the total specification width. For one-sided specifications, only Cpk can be calculated. Figure 6.25 shows how this would look on a control chart.

The objective of all this work is to quantify our conformance to stated requirements, and by identifying the position with reference

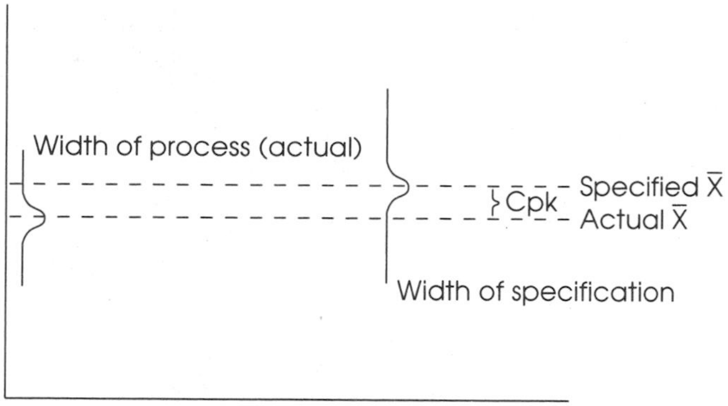

FIGURE 6.25 Control chart showing use of Cp and Cpk

to the target, and the variability of results, to determine if we are in compliance all the time, some of the time, or not at all.

Using this well-established procedure can also help us to continuously improve the situation, by providing concrete measurements of our progress. Yet it must be used in conjunction with other quality tools that will help identify sources of variability, allowing us to make improvements which can then be measured using control charts.

Summary

Charts in and of themselves are useless. Only when they are kept up-to-date, interpreted, and used as a guide in making adjustments will they be of any value. As the continuous improvement process takes place, control charts are updated to reflect the changing situation.

You may not see the need for control charts in personal matters, but even a simple measurement can help achieve personal goals. Regular measurement of weight in pounds and vigorous exercise in minutes could be handy tools to show their mutual effects on total weight, for example.

If you want to bring a process under tight control, you can do it using charts and graphs. Even if you don't know much about statistics, charting your actual facts can help you get started and monitor your progress. Gross changes will be obvious. As you get more sophisticated and need to draw finer distinctions, you will want to know more about statistics.

CONTROL TOOLS

While the conceptual tools were used to generate the original ideas, leading to an objective statement, and the analytical tools were used to better define the details, the control tools are used to keep track of progress and monitor results.

Control Charts

A well-respected organization, with a highly developed training program, flees from control charts. Why? To apply them in the strictest statistical sense, you need to have a lot of training. But the concept is simple and control charts can be used effectively with a reasonable amount of practice.

A control chart is a chart on which you show, usually over time, the results of your measurements. Its purpose is to help you observe trends and take corrective actions based on your measurements. That seems simple enough. Take your measurements on a regular basis, then write them down.

By doing just that much, you have accomplished a great deal. First, by taking the trouble to make the chart in the first place, you are demonstrating the importance of the thing you are measuring. Second, by taking measurements on a regular basis, you are developing a habit or discipline that will serve you in building your commitment to the matter at hand. Third, you are beginning to get an idea of the range of variation of your measurements.

In any process, you will either be trying to minimize something, maximize it, or create a trend toward some central point. In the case of minimizing or maximizing, you are trending toward some fixed endpoint (0 or 100 percent). Figure 6.26 shows examples of one-sided and two-sided control charts. For both minimizing and maximizing situations, the normal distribution may be skewed or bent as you approach the target.

The basic process of plotting performance, reviewing results, making adjustments, and moving forward can be powerful. Be

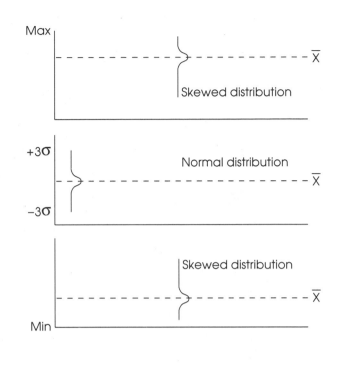

FIGURE 6.26 Basic control charts[12]

patient in learning the proper use of statistics. At the same time, don't let lack of detailed statistical knowledge prevent you from making a control chart. The first time you compute an average you are using statistics, and there's nothing scary about that. After all, the statement "Nothing worthwhile comes easily" applies very well to the field of statistics.

On a personal level, you may not need full-blown statistical analysis to determine your course of action. In may cases you can get a clear picture of what is happening without going any farther than putting your measurements on paper, computing an average, and observing the range of your data. The more money or time that are at stake, the more important it is to have solid data supported by solid statistics done by a competent practitioner. But there is a lot of useful ground between our first efforts and a doctorate in statistics. Here are a few examples.

In the Freddy's Machine Shop example, we had the start of a control chart. As you will recall, Freddy had charted his performance, analyzed his situation, increased his production to meet demand, and worked at decreasing his backlog. As a result of his efforts, business increased. In order to keep control of his situation, he must continue to use his run chart. But he needs a few refinements.

Recognizing that there will be some ebb and flow of incoming work, and that there will be some variation in his output rate due to vacations or illnesses, Freddy needs to establish some control limits that will let him know when to take corrective action. Let's start with customer requirements, as we did in the previous section.

Freddy's business increased when he brought his backlog under control. Let's say that by asking his customers he has established that the maximum acceptable wait time is half a day. His average incoming work is 30 per day, and he is now working at a rate of 32 per day, producing an average wait time of .47 day, or just under half a day. There is some variation in his output (process), however, and sometimes he slows down. He calculates his standard of deviation (sigma), which is approximately a quarter of a day. Figure 6.27 shows the results of his efforts. While the average is within acceptable limits, the variation is unacceptable.

In order to ensure compliance with customer satisfaction needs, Freddy must increase his capacity again. Assuming his variation remains the same, he must increase his capacity so that he rarely exceeds the customer wait requirement. This will cost money, but how much does it cost him in terms of lost business if he does not make the improvement? Now we're set up for a cost of quality question.

If Freddy does not use some form of statistics, he may guess right or he may not. By using his control chart and monitoring lost business, he can determine the most economical point at which to run.

I know a psychologist who tracks his business in a similar way. By collecting data over the years, he has established that incoming business is dependent on direct mail and other outside contact. If business is slow, he can increase his outside contact to increase business. Since he is aware of his costs, he has an excellent tool for

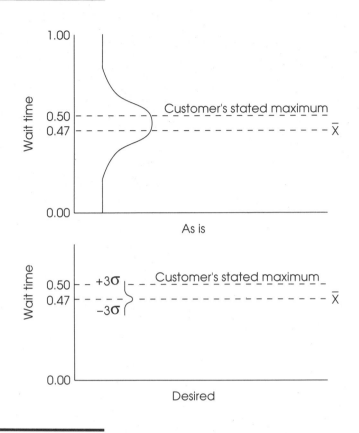

FIGURE 6.27 Freddy's machine control chart

controlling the pace of the business and its economics. He does not use a statistical control chart, but he tracks outside contacts and business level on a graph. He uses actual data to observe trends, but he does not do detailed statistics.

On a personal level, let's say that you have embarked on the ambitious task of learning how to play the piano. Your teacher has advised you that 30 minutes of practice daily will keep you up-to-date with the assigned lessons. You do this, and being statistically inclined, you time each practice session (weekends included) to the minute.

After a month of earnest study, you discover that both you and your teacher find your progress unacceptable. Unwilling to face

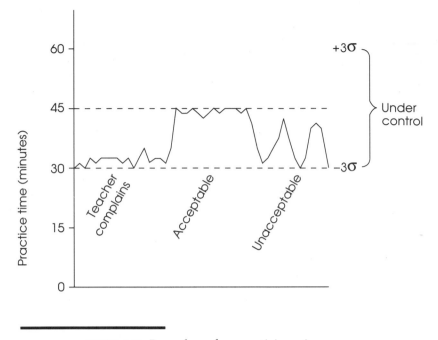

FIGURE 6.28 Run chart for practicing piano

the ridicule of your close friends (who bet you couldn't learn in the first place), you embark on your project with renewed vigor. You practice 45 minutes each day for a period of one week. Results are improved. This continues for a few weeks, with very acceptable results. After a certain period of time, like most piano students, you slack off a little, allowing yourself some freedom. Before you know it, you are reprimanded by your teacher for backsliding.

Searching furtively for a reasonable excuse seems folly, so you review your charts and find that over recent weeks you have had several days where you practiced only 30 minutes. Figure 6.28 shows the results. Even for simple activities, a run chart can be an effective tool. Only you can decide if it adds value.

Many skills, like playing the piano and typing, show major improvements as a direct result of practice. It seems that you must either increase your average minutes practiced to raise your whole curve up to the target level, or reduce your variance to prevent the bottom of the curve from dipping below the target.

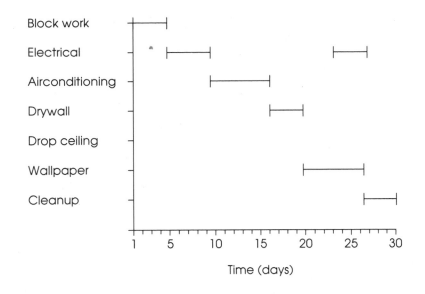

FIGURE 6.29 Gantt chart

The Gantt Chart

The Gantt chart is a more complicated form of the list. The value
it adds is that it puts the list in a time frame, and points to potential
areas of conflict. To construct a Gantt chart, list your activities
along the left margin and the time across the bottom of the page.
The time must provide for the full duration of the project (it may
take several pages), and the unit of measure should be the smallest
amount of time you would schedule. For example, a project might
take three months and you will check your progress daily. In this
case, you need a chart that will have roughly 90 columns, one for
each day in the three-month time requirement.

Figure 6.29 shows a Gantt chart that includes a list of activities
that must be completed during the construction of a room, but
they must be done in a particular sequence.

A Gantt chart is a simple but effective control tool. In the next
step, plan the project in order. This may mean that you reorganize
some steps to make it easy to see what comes next. One way to
do this is simply to organize your actions by starting date. For each

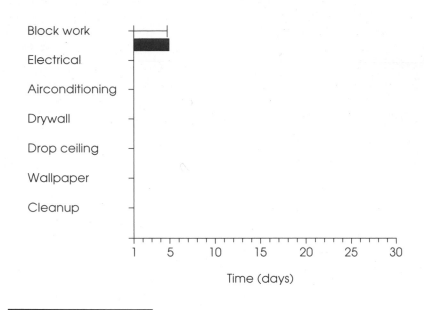

FIGURE 6.30 Gantt chart with progress shown

item, put a black line to extend from the starting date to the completion date for that item. It is alright for more than one item to happen at the same time, if you can manage them both.

As your project progresses, you will mark beside each bar your *actual start to finish* time, so you can track your project.

Figure 6.30 illustrates a technique for showing progress: achievements are shown in dark and targets in light.

Cost of Quality

No discussion of quality improvement is truly complete without a comment on the subject of the cost of quality. Crosby popularized the phrase "quality is free." Later on, he refined the idea, when he said that quality is free, but it's not a gift.[13] The fact is, we must usually work hard to improve quality. But when you've taken a step, you will usually find that it is easier to do something right the first time than to allow variation, failures, and rejects, then go back and fix them.

Major companies have found after detailed investigations that the cost of poor quality is a significant part of their overhead expense. Study of the cost of poor quality can be complicated, but even so, the concept is simple. Here's a brief and basic example of cost of quality analysis, frequently called a quality cost audit.

In Company X, staff are complaining about the number of errors in material charge-out slips. A slip must be filled out properly every time material is taken out of the stock room. After months of frustration, Judy, who makes the corrections for these errors, totalled the time spent just on corrections and found that it took her three hours a day. It took her about 10 minutes for each item she had to correct, including identifying the specific problem, finding the correct part number (or other item), reversing the original transaction, creating the new transaction, and then checking the computer printout the following day to ensure that all transactions were done correctly. She borrowed a stopwatch and timed the process of writing the original charge-out slip, including stopping to look up the part number in the warehouse listing. It took three minutes.

Although it seems obvious that it is better to do something in three minutes than in 10 minutes, changing the situation may not be simple. Frequently, changes in awareness, trust, and cooperation within an organization must occur before improvements can be made. If the building of trust and cooperation were a simple process, more people would be doing it. In later chapters, we will offer tools for working with groups and organizations.

When working on your own projects, interpersonal issues, such as building trust, are not barriers. Here's an example of cost of poor quality on a personal basis.

For some time now, you have wanted to establish a savings program. You knew from your general reading that it is more economical to spend what you have than to purchase on credit, but you could never seem to get a handle on it. You decide to perform a cost of quality audit on your purchasing behavior.

You list each credit purchase in one column and each cash purchase in the other column. In the credit column, you also document fees paid each month for interest and other credit charges. At the end of one full month, you review the results. Figure 6.31 shows a likely example and you find that it is costing you an average of 6 percent a month to have credit.

	CREDIT	CASH
	100.	50.
	45.	60.
	25.	10.
Interest	20.	
	65.	75.
	75.	35.
	20.	40.
Subtotal cost	330.	
Credit cost	20.	
Totals	350.	270.

Monthly cost of credit (poor quality?) = 20/350 = 6%

FIGURE 6.31 Cost of quality for individual purchases

After weighing the additional convenience against the extra 6 percent, you decide to change your behavior. Recognizing that it is unrealistic to eliminate your credit purchases totally, you set aside $30 per month to pay on your credit until the balance is zero. At that point, you have a savings program and you have developed a habit.

Your "cost of poor quality" was $20 per month, 6 percent of credit purchases or a little over 3 percent of all purchases. You are now in a position to monitor your cost of poor quality on a continuing basis, eventually reducing it to zero.

Any activity, at home or at work, that does not add some value is wasted. That may seem like a rigid statement, yet if you can use this concept to improve your quality of work or life, so much the better.

The Checklist

Last, but not least, is the checklist, discussed earlier; the simplest and most practical universal tool in the quality improvement toolbox. If this is all that is required, then it's all that should be used.

APPRAISAL (SELF-EVALUATION)

All our lives, we are evaluated by other people: first by our parents, then by teachers, then by bosses or supervisors, perhaps by a minister or priest, and certainly by our friends and colleagues. In fact, we are so used to being evaluated by others that we may forget to evaluate ourselves. In order to do an evaluation, we need three prerequisites:

1. A set of goals or objectives
2. Some structure for evaluation
3. An open attitude to self-criticism

In the first few chapters of this book, we talked about setting goals. You probably have some firm goals in mind already. If you have been practicing along the way, you may have some specific indicators which can be measured.

You don't need a Gantt chart for self-evaluation, but it might help. How often will you check your progress? What is your personal schedule? When do you expect to make that second million? You can use the tools we have just discussed to put together your personal program.

The most difficult part of the self-evaluation process is preparing yourself to accept your own criticism. To do this, you must strike a balance between criticism and acceptance. If you are too hard on yourself, you can become demoralized. If you are too accepting of shortfalls, then you won't accomplish anything. So you need to find the happy medium between being too harsh and too lenient. This will enable you to achieve continuous improvement.

Each time you improve something, that's cause for celebration. Even a small improvement can make a difference. As long as you are headed in the right direction, and keep headed in the right direction, you will be ahead of the game. If that's not enough, then redefine your requirements and go for more.

One popular way to visualize this process is that of a never-ending circle of planning, doing, checking what you have done, and adjusting (P-D-C-A, or the Deming cycle). As our control of personal processes improves, the circle can be thought of as getting smaller as we make one improvement after another. When the circle is small enough (as determined by our indicators), we start another cycle in some other area. By keeping our original indicators in place, we will always know if a process gets out of control. We accomplish this control with a minimum of effort, just by staying in touch with the relevant facts (checking our indicators).

All the tools we have talked about so far require no outside help, and can be practiced on your own. But if you wish to communicate your accomplishments to others, or to explain your process so that it can be applied elsewhere, it will be helpful to have an organized way to do this. That's where the quality improvement story comes in handy.

THE QUALITY IMPROVEMENT STORY

The quality improvement story has been developed over the years as a tool for describing quality improvement successes to others in a way that the actions and the logic can be easily understood.

One of the biggest hurdles to overcome is to define for others what is obvious to us. When you have been involved in a project for a long time or very intensely, it is hard to keep in mind that others know nothing of your activities. If you do not explain clearly, logically, and concisely what you have done, your chances of a warm reception grow slim.

In the example that follows, the development of one story is shown from start to finish. The strength of the story technique is that it is designed to show each part of the process logically and in turn, using standard charts and graphs. Because most people like a good story, especially one they can understand, the story method is an excellent way to share your successes with others.

For an example, let's use our original personal improvement objectives and observe how a quality improvement story might unfold. Please take special note at the way the graphic tools enable even the casual reader to focus on the key points.

Sample Quality Improvement Story

Step One: Problem Identification

Present activities are not organized around our objective statement, resulting in misallocation of resources and feelings of uselessness.

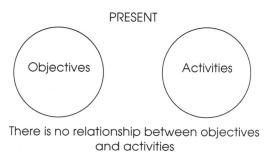

PRESENT

There is no relationship between objectives
and activities

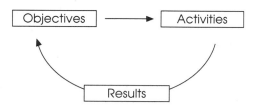

DESIRED

Objectives should drive activities; activities should then reinforce objectives.

Step Two: Problem Analysis

Brainstorming helped to identify 50 areas of interest. These were then narrowed down to the four which were most deserving of attention: starting a savings plan, eliminating bad habits, getting into shape, and learning to play the piano. Feeling useful to others (identified earlier as a potential area of improvement) was viewed as a result, not an activity.

Visualization of our goals led us to adopt the Fuller objective as the objective statement of this project. Each proposed action was evaluated according to its estimated benefit to the four criteria, as shown in Table 6.9. According to our analysis, getting rid of bad habits was the most useful project to begin with.

	PROTECTION/ SUPPORT	REMOVE CONSTRAINTS	IMPROVE INITIATIVE	TOTAL
Habits	10	3.3	3.3	16.6
Communication	10	10	5	15.0
Revised	0	5	9	14.0
Toolbox	0	4	10	14.0

TABLE 6.9 Final evaluation matrix

The Five Whys were used to test the results of the matrix. Only three were required:

1. The objective of this project is to rid myself of the bad habits of smoking and eating too many doughnuts. Why?
2. Because these habits are preventing me from accomplishing my major objectives. Why?
3. Because they take time away from other activities, diminish my personal capacity, and have a direct negative impact on others. Why?

This last why took us directly back to our objective statement, which has already been accepted and has held up against similar questioning.

Step Three: Planning

Two specific actions need to be corrected: smoking and eating. Cost of poor quality was used to evaluate potential actions. Based on the analysis shown in Table 6.10, smoking is the first habit to work on.

There were several potential indicators: number of packs smoked, cost of cigarettes, number and cost of doctor visits and medication, and estimated lost time (which is a function of packs smoked).

Two options were considered: the zero defects approach which would bring smoking to zero, or a less aggressive approach to bring smoking down below doughnuts as the high cost of quality

	SMOKING	DOUGHNUTS
Direct cost (per year)	$520	$156
Estimated additional costs		
Doctor visits	$120	
New clothes (weight increase)		$600
Estimated lost time (at 30 min/day $15/hr)	$2,737	
Total Annual Cost	$3,377	$756

TABLE 6.10 Cost of poor quality comparison

item. Recognizing that results will likely be in proportion to goals, the first approach, zero defects, was selected.

Step Four: Data Collection
Figure 6.32 was constructed and present activity was plotted. The data indicate a pack-a-day habit.

Step Five: Data Interpretation
To determine the root cause, the habit was reviewed from several points of view: time of day, association with other activities, triggers, and alternatives. Root cause was determined to be that the person in question (I) never had sufficient motivation to overcome the habit (Figure 6.33).

A variety of countermeasures were considered. The most effective countermeasure was to identify this project with the key goals of the person's overall objective statement.

Information to facilitate the withdrawal process, possibly including a professionally administered program, represents another set of countermeasures.

There is a procedural countermeasure: Do not smoke.

Finally, self-praise was used to facilitate the process. Recognizing the need to continually reinforce our change, we planned to do this on a daily basis.

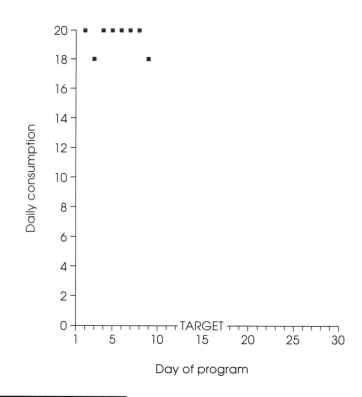

FIGURE 6.32 Run chart showing a pack-a-day habit

Step Six: Action

A suitable, professionally administered program was selected. Cost was easily justified because it was less than one year's cost of poor quality. Results were tracked using the original chart (Figure 6.34). A significant reduction in smoking was achieved.

Step Seven: Appraisal

Data showed substantial improvement, although the target had not yet been met.

Follow-up options (future plans) include continuing with this project until zero defects is reached, continuing this project while initiating another, and discontinuing this project in favor of the one with the new highest cost or gain. Knowing my personal limitations, I elected to continue with this project to zero defects, while investigating alternatives for the next project.

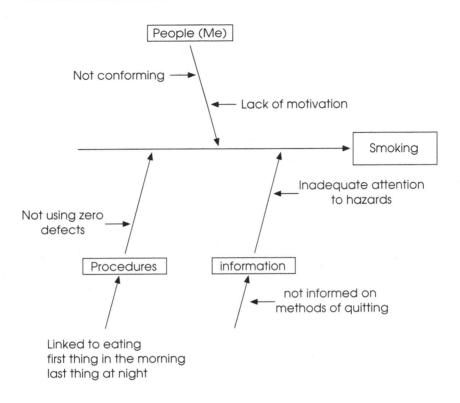

FIGURE 6.33 Fishbone analysis of smoking behavior

THE FINAL ANALYSIS

There are many ways to accomplish almost any goal. In the final analysis, however, action must be taken before results can be achieved. Some people are blessed with the unique ability to make a quick decision and proceed until they have accomplished their goal. Others accomplish their objectives in a gradual way. Organized thinking, structured problem-solving techniques, and good use of information are all tools which are readily available for our use. Obstacles may very well be only within ourselves. The examples in this chapter, both large-scale (Fuller objective) and small-scale (changing a personal habit) show that quality tools can

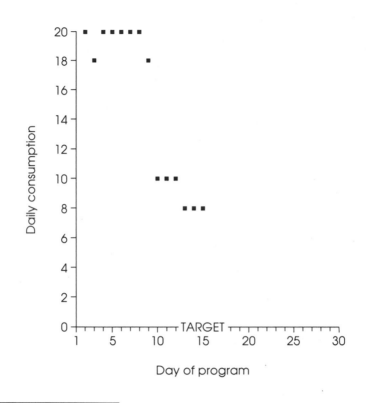

FIGURE 6.34 Run Chart Showing Improvements

be used in an organized way to identify and overcome obstacles in your quest for personal change.

In order to begin the process, one needs only to ask the following questions:

Who am I? Define your specific requirements.

Where am I in the process of change? Recognize that change is a continual process.

Where do I want to start the improvement process? Select your area of improvement.

Then do it. Apply quality improvement tools to your personal processes.

References

1. Hansen, Mark Victor. *Future Diary*. Newport Beach, CA: Mark Victor Hansen Publishing Co., 1980.

2. Juran, J. M. *Juran on Planning for Quality*. New York: Free Press, 1988, 18–20.

3. The Phillips Phlowchart was taken in concept from 1984 conversations with Richard W. Phillips, a manager at Tampa Armature Works, in which he expressed his exasperation over a confused "system."

4. *Quality Improvement Story and Techniques*. Miami: Florida Power and Light, 1987, 40.

5. Budnick, Frank S., Richard Mojena, and Thomas E. Vollman. *Principles of Operations Research for Management*. Homewood, IL: Richard D. Irwin, 1977, 441.

6. Mizuno, Shigeru, ed. *Management for Quality Improvement*. Cambridge, MA: Productivity Press, 1979.

7. Juran, J. M., and Frank M. Gryna. *Quality Planning and Analysis*. New York: McGraw-Hill, 1980, 101–102.

8. Juran, J. M. "The Non-Pareto Principle; Mea Culpa." *Quality Progress* 8, (May 1975): 8–9.

9. Stigler, Stephen M. *The History of Statistics*. Cambridge, MA: Belknap Press of Harvard University Press, 1986, 139–143.

10. Besterfield, Dale H. *Quality Control*. Englewood Cliffs, NJ: Prentice-Hall, 1986, 85.

11. Juran, J. M., and Frank M. Gryna. *Quality Control Handbook* Fourth Edition. New York: McGraw-Hill, 1988, 24.33.

12. Juran, J. M., and Frank M. Gryna. *Quality Control Handbook* Fourth Edition. New York: McGraw-Hill, 1988, 24.34–35.

13. Crosby, Philip, B. *Quality Is Free*. New York: McGraw-Hill, 1979, 15–23.

Suggested Reading

Besterfield, Dale H. *Quality Control.* Englewood Cliffs, NJ: Prentice-Hall, 1986.

Crosby, Philip, B. *Quality Is Free.* New York: McGraw-Hill, 1979.

Deming, W. Edwards. *Out of Crisis.* Cambridge, MA: Massachusetts Institute of Technology, 1986.

Ishikawa, Kaoru. *What Is Total Quality Control?* Englewood Cliffs, NJ: Prentice-Hall, 1985.

Juran, J. M., and Frank M. Gryna, Jr. *Quality Planning and Analysis.* New York: McGraw-Hill, 1980.

Juran, J. M., Frank M. Gryna, Jr. *Quality Control Handbook* Fourth Edition. New York: McGraw-Hill, 1988.

Mizuno, Shigeru, ed. *Management for Quality Improvement.* Cambridge, MA: Productivity Press, 1979.

Schrock Edward M., and Henry L. Lefevre. *The Good and the Bad News About Quality.* Milwaukee: ASQC Quality Press, 1988.

Seven

FROM THE INDIVIDUAL TO THE GROUP

So far, we have discussed the seven-step quality improvement process, the five stages of personal change, and provided specific quality tools that can be applied to almost any personal project to improve its chances of success. But we have not yet talked about how to get outside your own head and begin to work with others. Working with other people requires additional skills and practices. These skills and practices deal more with feelings than facts, more with intangibles than tangibles, and have come from the areas of psychology, communications, human relations, and organizational development.

If we look at the development of relationships as a process, and if we identify the stages of this process through which we must pass, we can then simplify and organize our work of introducing change to another individual, group, or organization. In other words, a knowledge of quality tools and personal change is not enough to get something done outside yourself. You need to develop relationships. One of the most basic concepts in communications is personal integrity. Crosby mentions this in his book, *Quality Without Tears,* in the context of management behavior.[1] Yet it is just as valuable a concept to anyone.

When we communicate with others, we do it in four ways: listening, talking, writing, and body language. In addition, we communicate on two levels: explicitly (thoughts) and implicitly (feelings). When our talking, writing, and body language do not agree with one another, or when our explicit and implicit communications are at conflict, we lack integrity or wholeness. The irony is that others frequently see this in us before we are aware of it in ourselves.

One of the reasons that we went into such depth about the planning portion of improvement was to provide the opportunity to think through our actions so that we can be comfortable with our decisions, and therefore possess personal integrity. The seven-step process takes care of the explicit or thought part of the equation, but we must also be aware of the feeling side.

Business in general has frequently presented the image of an unemotional machine conducting transactions without regard to the people involved. Expressions such as "business-like" and "strictly business" communicate this idea. The fact is that many business leaders are acutely aware of the feelings as well as the thoughts of their associates. By taking feelings into consideration, they make both themselves and their associates into winners, because the leaders put their associates into positions where their thoughts and feelings will be useful to the organization. They actually help create integrity.

There is nothing more important than integrity in getting through to others. It has frequently been said that most business is done over a handshake. In my experience, that has been true. The only way this long tradition is preserved is by the constant development and reinforcement of a culture in which "a person is only as good as their word"[2] (another way of defining integrity). If you want quality improvement methods to be practiced in your group, you must first use them consistently yourself. Equally important, when you say that you're going to do something, *do it.* Every time. No excuses. Personal integrity is the cornerstone of good communications. Care for it well.

Building from your cornerstone of personal integrity, you can apply communications skills to further the practice of quality improvement techniques in your organization.

Self-respect is frequently called the first requirement of good interpersonal communications. By resolving your personal conflicts by positive use of the change process, you can contribute to respect for yourself. Self-respect makes it easier to have respect for others, and this provides a solid basis for communications with others.

Respect in itself is still not enough to complete the process. The next step is understanding yourself and the other person. It is possible to respect someone without understanding them, but to achieve effective communications, we must understand, both explicitly and implicitly, from where we and they are coming. How?

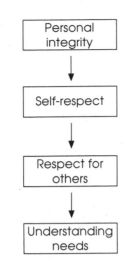

FIGURE 7.1 Flowchart for developing relationships

They will tell us. We just have to learn to listen to ourselves and others, and be aware of what we hear.

Finally, we can apply our understanding to the accomplishment of specific tasks, using effective communications to bridge the gap from ourselves to others.

Figure 7.1 shows a flowchart of the process of developing and improving relationships.

UNDERSTANDING BEHAVIOR STYLES

Armed with your solid base of personal integrity and with your quality toolbox in hand, you are now ready to work with your associates to accomplish your improvement goals. There are two ways to do this—the hard way and the easier way. The hard way is to push your ideas through the organization without regard for other people's feelings about the issues. In this case, you may succeed in the short term, but can probably expect that in a relatively short time your associates will see to it that your project will fail. The easier way is to educate yourself regarding the feelings of your associates, drawing on their strengths to help you along, and working on problem areas before they threaten your whole idea.

One tool which is helpful in understanding others is the behavior style analysis. This is done effectively by Cathcart and Alessandra.[3] By understanding each person's behavior style we can tailor our discussions with them so they will be receptive to our ideas, each in her or his own way. In Cathcart and Alessandra's analysis, the four primary types or styles are relaters, socializers, thinkers, and directors. By understanding which type you are, you can more realistically check your strengths and weaknesses, and set about forming teams with people who will complement you, having strengths where you have weaknesses. By understanding which type your associates are, you can make sure you talk to them in language that they understand and to which they respond. Behavior style can have an important effect on interpersonal communications.[4] Figure 7.2 gives some ideas about each type.

Infinite Variability

Although the styles we just discussed are useful, we should be aware that everyone is an individual, perhaps having elements of all four types.

That's even better, but we still haven't accounted for all the variability among individuals. This is where listening skills come to the fore. In Zig Ziglar's sales training tapes,[5] he talks about the importance of listening. He points out that your customer (or associate) will tell you what you need to do . . . all you have to do is be alert and listen to what he says.

One useful approach to quality in relationships, which I first heard used by Florida Power and Light employees, is that anyone can be your "customer." In other words, we can think of another person as if we were the proprietors of a store and they have come to purchase something. For example, I give reports to my boss, therefore he is my customer. He provides me with guidance and direction (on which I place a value), so I am his customer. To this extent, Ziglar's tapes can apply to any interaction. Watch the body language of your customer, and listen to what the other person

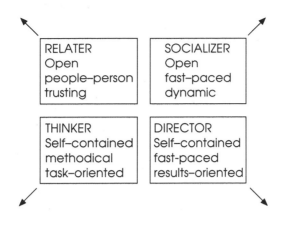

FIGURE 7.2 Four basic behavior styles

says. Ask questions if you don't understand. If you ask the right question they may tell you exactly what you need to know.

Although behavior styles can be useful in understanding behavior in general, there is an infinite variability from one person to another, and we should avoid the danger of stereotyping somebody in a particular category. People are individuals, and may have in-between traits.[6]

YOUR PLACE IN THE ORGANIZATION

Regardless of your behavior style or ideals, your actions will be partly determined by your position in the organization. You can use specific skills to bring your program to each individual, based on your relationship within the structure of the organization. Figure 7.3 summarizes the types of relationships normally present in an organization.

Your Subordinates

If you are a supervisor or manager, some people report directly or indirectly to you. Experience has proven that these people are

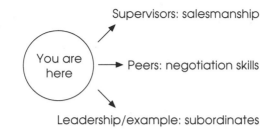

Supervisors: salesmanship

You are here → Peers: negotiation skills

Leadership/example: subordinates

FIGURE 7.3 Interpersonal skills

looking to you for leadership. If you do nothing else but stick to your own regimen, setting a positive example, you are off to a good start. If you actively encourage your subordinates to talk to you and to share their ideas, that's even better. If you actually give them the opportunity to implement their ideas, that's even better. But most importantly, your subordinates are looking to you to set the pace and the example. That's where the personal integrity becomes crucial. If you aren't sold on what you are doing, no one else will be either.

Your Peers

Anyone on the same level in the organization that you are is your peer. That means they either report to the same supervisor you do, report to somebody at the same level as your supervisor, or have a roughly similar situation to you in spite of the reporting relationships.

At this level, your negotiating skills are important. Setting an example is still useful, but these people are not looking to you for leadership. Your leadership is the result of your interest in an issue. Because it depends on your role in the situation rather than on your authority in the organization, it is called situational leadership. Another way to describe this situation is to say that your authority is based on your integrity, your personality, and your competence rather than your position in the organization. You are the leader until responsibility is taken for your project by someone else.[7]

In order to enter into a negotiation, both parties must have something to gain or lose. If this precondition does not exist, there can be no negotiation.

Remember that these people are entering the process at *Step One: Problem Identification*. In other words, they are thinking about something else or someone else when you come into their office with your ideas. You will need to make them comfortable with you, and provide them with information before you can talk about how you can work together.

Supervisors

Supervisors or managers to whom you report will require yet another approach. Everybody wants something from them. So you have to put on your sales hat and use salesmanship to get through to them. Since they are busy with other things, you have to be concise and fight for your piece of their time. We will deal with changing management attitudes in a later chapter. For now, it is enough to know that you can draw on four areas of skill to deal with others in your organization:

1. Behavior styles
2. Leadership
3. Negotiation
4. Salesmanship

Although each can be used at any time and place, you can expect to use them as shown in Figure 7.3. The reason you will expect to see these themes predominate has to do with the relationships established within the organization.

With your supervisors, you will frequently be vying against your peers for use of limited resources, particularly if you are attempting to implement a change. You will have to sell your concepts effectively if you want to liberate those resources for your use. Another way to define *sell* is to present your concept in its best possible light.

With your peers, you will frequently require their cooperation because many opportunities for change require more than one person. Both you and they must have something to gain or lose in order for a negotiation to occur. You will need to show them how they can gain by adopting your recommended change. You may also have to give up something in order to get something in return. So you negotiate.

Last, but in no way least, your subordinates may use you as an example, whether you like it or not. People working under my supervision have made it crystal clear to me that even slight (to me) variations in my behavior make a big difference to them. Imagine the importance, then, of daily actions that support your program or act to nullify it.

THE FIVE STAGES OF CHANGE

Regardless of which group or personality type you are working with, you will be catching them in *Stage One: Recognition of the Need for Change*. So, to start out, you must give them the same information that led you to the idea that change is needed. You must also do something else. You must shepherd them through the stages of change, which are as follows:

- Denial
- Anger
- Negotiation
- Depression
- Acceptance

Different types of people will handle stages in different ways, but each person must get through the entire process before you can go on to apply quality improvement tools to a situation. You may wish to use the story technique to present this information. The way you tell your story can have an affect on the way it is received.

For instance, I know a manager who could be described as a Director. If I plan to recommend a change to a procedure which he views as in control, I had better be sure I have the data to show that it is not in control. It may be hard for him to accept that his control system is not working as planned. He may get to the anger stage, and I could be the unwilling object of that anger. By telling a story, explaining how I became curious about the situation, and providing room for a face-saving response by this director, I may avoid an unfriendly encounter.

Timing of the presentation is important. Ask when it would be convenient for you to discuss a certain issue. He may tell you. Watch the reactions to the first few statements. If it is going negative, you may wish to stop and ask, "Does this make sense to you?" or "How does this sound so far?"

There are as many ways of looking at people as there are people to look at. Each approach has its positive points. For our purposes, we must understand where we are and where the other person is, in the process of change. We must complete the process together if we are to proceed on a specific task.

Figure 7.4 shows how this whole process fits together. In concept, you start down your individual path to change a specific thing, you go through your five stages of change, developing a commitment to action, you apply the seven-step quality improvement process to the issue at hand, you identify others in your organization who must participate if you are to succeed. Taking into consideration the type of person you are dealing with, and your relationship to this person in the organization, you apply the tools of salesmanship, negotiation, and example, to the interaction as they may apply. This enables you to bring the other person or persons into the process along with you. You then work together to define the directions you wish to go together and begin the seven-step process as a team. The personal process of change is only the start of quality improvement in an organization. Specific organizational tools must be used as well.

Here's an example. You have decided to improve your physical health by implementing a personal exercise program. You reason that if this is a good idea for you, it is probably a good idea for everybody, so you approach Bruce, personnel manager, with the idea. By observing your general condition, Bruce pays the obligatory amount of attention to you and forgets the issue entirely.

You go back to analyze the situation, and decide that you have diluted the integrity of your position by not having practiced a physical conditioning regime yourself. Applying your basic quality improvement tools, you achieve a modest improvement in your physical appearance, and return to Bruce with the product of your efforts. This time the reception is different.

Bruce, however, has his own set of problems. You ask a few open questions and do a lot of listening. Bruce explains that he has

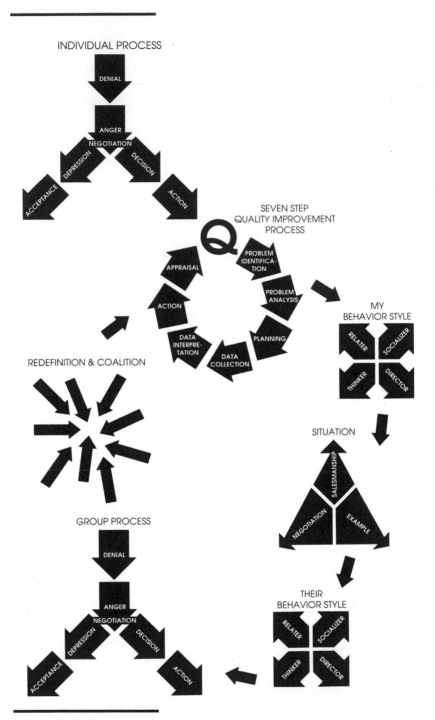

FIGURE 7.4

certain budget constraints, and other programs must take precedence. Now, you have something with which to work. What are the constraints? What are the other programs? What are the budgetary benefits of your program in terms of lowered lost-time accidents, reduced health insurance, and other benefits?

Having collected a good amount of information from other similar programs, you return to Bruce (armed this time with charts and graphs) and show the benefits of your program. Now you are selling and you may yet have to negotiate to get a part of your program in place.

Up to this point, we have gone through the process of personal change, produced personal change (using the quality improvement tools), communicated this change to the personnel manager, and identified his stage in the process of change. You have treated him as a customer, listening to his problems and objections, and used the new information which he provided as a guidepost for building your case. You are also prepared to negotiate to gain some improvement rather than none at all.

Now, you are prepared to develop a coalition with Bruce, to identify company needs and to work together to produce change which will be useful to other people. You can then apply the seven-step problem-solving process to the new goals.

Place this example in the context of an organization in a continual state of change, and you have a real-world example.

SUMMARY

Expanding our ideas to other people involves a variety of skills, each taking some time to learn. But each skill has its place in the overall picture of improvement. We all start out with very few skills, and build as we go. Your personal improvement process, applied to your own goals, will show you where to put your energies. The farther you want to expand your influence, the more skills you will need. Each skill area is a discipline unto itself. Don't be impatient. Just keep making steady forward progress.

References

1. Crosby, Philip B. *Quality Without Tears*. New York: New American Library, 1984, 8.

2. This is a statement which was made by the father of a friend. I must have been about 10 years old when I heard it said, but have never forgotten it. Since that time, experience has proved this statement true to me. I can't attribute this to a particular culture or religion, but I do know that much business is still done on a handshake.

3. Alessandra, Tony, and Jim Cathcart. *Relationship Strategies*. Chicago: Nightingale-Conant, 1990.

4. Alessandra, Tony, and Jim Cathcart. *Relationship Strategies*. Chicago: Nightingale-Conant, 1990.

5. Ziglar, Zig. *Sell Your Way to the Top*. Chicago: Nightingale-Conant, 1990.

6. Alessandra, Tony, and Jim Cathcart. *Relationship Strategies*. Chicago: Nightingale-Conant, 1990.

7. Jongaeward, Dorothy, ed. *Everybody Wins*. Reading, MA: Addison-Wesley, 1973, 67.

Suggested Reading

Nirenberg, Jesse S. *Getting Through to People*. Englewood Cliffs, NJ: Prentice-Hall, 1989.

Tichy, Noel M., and Mary Anne Devanna. *The Transformational Leader*. New York: John Wiley and Sons, 1990.

Section Three

GROUP INVOLVEMENT

Eight

BUILDING
A CONSTITUENCY

In order to get elected, a politician must first build a constituency, or a group of followers. Even if we're not running for office, we frequently need support for our ideas or activities. This is where your constituency becomes important. There are two parts to this job: effective communications, and encouragement of others. Using the overview shown in Figure 7.4, let's look at some of the basic skills we will need to get our ideas across to other people.

INTERPERSONAL COMMUNICATIONS

Communicating with others is done in four ways: listening, talking, writing, and nonverbal or body language. Further, we communicate in both thoughts and feelings. If we have personal integrity, our thoughts, actions, and words will all combine to communicate our ideas to others.

Listening

Xerox made listening a hot issue when they built a whole program around this concept.[1] Believe it or not, it is hard to listen. In his book *Getting Through to People,* Jesse Nirenberg points out some of the other things we do when we're supposed to be listening.[2] One is that we're really waiting for our turn to talk. That is quite different from listening. If we are just waiting for our turn to talk, we are thinking about what we will say next, not about what is being said. As a result, we frequently ignore or misunderstand what the other person is saying.

A second thing we do is think about other things. When we're thinking about other things, we're totally distracted and have no idea what's going on.

A third problem is in talking too much. In doing this, we deny ourselves the opportunity to listen. Frequently a person will ask for a moment of your time to share an experience or thought with you. The next thing they know, they're listening to an oration having nothing to do with the original subject. To overcome this obstacle, we must be sensitive to the other person's objective in talking to us. Turning this concept around, it is our job to make sure that the other person is sensitive to our needs.

One way to encourage someone is to ask questions. This clearly shows that you have heard them and are thinking about what they are saying. Asking the right questions is important, too. What you ask can frequently determine the value you get out of your conversation with the other person.

Talking

Talking probably gets us into more trouble than it gets us out of. We talk in two ways, with our mouths and with our bodies.

Body Language

Many people pay more attention to body language than to what you actually say. I think there's a song that says "it ain't what you say, it's how you say it." This is the most common way people get caught in a lie, fib, or exaggeration. They say the right words, but not in the right way. That's why it's so important to be honest with yourself and others. Sooner or later, if you are not, you'll get caught. The most common things to watch for in ourselves and others are: eyes looking down and to the side, shifting in the chair, and an uneven speech pattern. These items are frequently signs that something is not right.

Talking

Verbal communication is probably the easiest part to master, as there are more opportunities to practice. Here are a few tips:

- Praise in public, criticize in private.
- Keep it simple.
- Think first, talk later.
- In humor, tease yourself, not others.
- Never use poor, foul, or offensive language.
- Keep it friendly, don't take things personally.

Writing

The most important thing from a quality standpoint is to never write when you can talk to a person eyeball-to-eyeball. When you do write, be careful how to say things. Imagine your memo on the front page of the newspaper. That will probably keep you out of trouble. And never write something negative about another person. Constituencies can't be built on negatives.

Energy Level

The pace at which you move projects forward, and your overall energy level are an important part of your nonverbal communications. Be aware of the way you appear to others. To put this another way, if you don't put your personal energy into a project, how can you expect someone else to contribute theirs?

Thinking versus Feeling

Women are often praised for being better at expressing their feelings than men. Yet we all need to express our feelings, each in our own way. In spite of which level we are most comfortable with, we are all working on both levels all the time. Be sensitive to both levels, and you will communicate much more effectively. Watch for the other person's body language and tone of voice. Listen for changes which reflect their feelings. Listen to yourself, too.

ENCOURAGEMENT OF OTHERS

Consider the person's position in your group. They may expect a little extra care or respect if they are in a senior position. Better still, why not treat everybody with respect and save a lot of needless decision-making?

When we learn a new technique or idea, we are frequently so excited that we want to tell everybody, and share our excitement. This can sometimes backfire if we are not careful how we approach others. Among the most important concepts is to make use of *their* ideas, by listening to them and encouraging them.

Bob Henderson, a professor at the University of South Florida, taught a course on management. Since I already had several years of experience in this area, I perhaps did not give the extra effort required to distinguish myself. . . . Until one day, at an association meeting, Dr. Henderson referred to me as one of his outstanding students. Although up to that point I had not been outstanding, by making the statement, he made me want to live up to it. Dr. Henderson gave me these words of wisdom, which I have not forgotten:

> Praise in public, criticize in private. Treat complaints and criticism with dignity.[3]

When you have practiced all the techniques we've discussed, you will find that you can build a constituency (a group of people who will support you in your projects) because you listened to them, made use of their ideas, and treated them with respect. By doing this, you helped them to be successful in their own right.

THE EXCEPTION TO THE RULE

Although the information presented so far may be useful, it does not cover all behavior. Not everybody responds uniformly to fair treatment, and we are never perfect in our communications with others, no matter how hard we try. Sometimes people just don't respond the way we would like them to and that's what the next chapter is about.

References

1. Crosby, Philip B. *Running Things*. New York: McGraw-Hill, 1986, 36–37.

2. Nirenberg, Jesse S. *Getting Through to People*. Englewood Cliffs, NJ: Prentice-Hall, 1989.

3. Robert D. Henderson, adjunct professor, University of South Florida. Material was drawn from conversations related to management teaching in 1985.

Suggested Readings

Bramson, Robert. *Coping with Difficult People.* New York: Dell Publishing Group, 1981.

Nirenberg, Jesse S. *Getting Through to People.* Englewood Cliffs, NJ: Prentice-Hall, 1989.

Suarez, R., Roger C. Mills, and Darlene Stuart. *Sanity, Insanity and Common Sense.* New York: Fawcett-Columbine (Balentine), 1980.

Nine

INDIVIDUAL BEHAVIORS IN THE GROUP

People are social animals. In spite of some notable exceptions to the rule (you may know some of them) most of us interact amicably on a daily basis. We socialize with each other in some very basic ways that are rooted in our animal nature. An understanding of some of these basic behaviors can be helpful in working with others in an organization, and also in building teams. Three of the most common types of behaviors are mounting behavior, grooming behavior, and manipulation. These behaviors may be observed in bosses, peers, or subordinates.

Regardless of our own philosophy of the way people should behave toward one another, these behaviors exist. Viewing them as a simple animal component of our behavior has helped me understand why people do the things they do. Here are a few of the most common examples.

MOUNTING BEHAVIORS

Mounting behavior is easy to find in animals. With people, it is sometimes shown in more subtle ways. If you are on the lookout for these behaviors, you don't have to wait too long to see them in the workplace. To start with, let's take an imaginary trip to the zoo. We amble past the primates: monkeys, apes, or chimps. From time to time, one will climb up on the back of another. Sometimes it looks like a sexual act, but it is usually not; it is mounting behavior. This is the way one animal shows dominance over another. You may say that these are animals, not people. True, yet have you ever heard the expression, "Get off my back?" When one person acts in a way to "put another person down" (another mounting expression), particularly in the presence of others, this is mounting behavior. It is that person's attempt to express dominance. In earlier generations, this was acceptable management behavior.[1] In much of today's business and social environment, it is viewed as nonproductive behavior. Since we have all been raised with a certain amount of this in our background, it is not surprising that almost everybody still shows this behavior at least occasionally. You may accept this behavior from your boss, but you probably don't enjoy it. From others, you may not accept it at all. You know when it's being done to you, because it is an obvious put-down. But it is easier to understand when you are aware that this person is trying to express dominance (where it may, or may not exist). Aside from the basic put-down, here are some other mounting behaviors.

The Good–Old Fashioned Stab in the Back

Some people, after years of solid relationships, can be totally honest and up-front, but most of our relationships are not that strong. At the same time, there are many opportunities to discuss situations outside of the chain of command. Let's face it, nobody's perfect. If you want to be in a winning situation, you can't fight this fire with fire. It only puts you in an equally bad light. A few ways to overcome this are as follows:

- Encourage up-front communications.
- Avoid stabbing others in the back.
- Use facts to counter unfair accusations.

Sniping

Sniping works in business just like it does in guerilla war. The sniper hides from a convenient vantage point, and takes easy shots at targets of convenience (this could be you). You can't avoid the sniper on any given occasion, but you can turn the tables and ask the sniper for a constructive suggestion. The worst you can get out of the encounter is a suggestion for improvement. As a result of smoking him or her out, you gain control of the situation.

Back-Shooting

This is particularly negative behavior, because it can have worse results for the person who does it than on the victim. It works like this. A decision needs to be made, but your associate does not want to take the risk of being wrong. So he or she delays until you must make the decision. If it turns out to be right, he or she says nothing. If it turns out to be wrong, he or she criticizes you for the decision. The best defense against this technique is to get the input of other interested parties (and bosses in particular) before making a final decision. The person is not then in a position to criticize the decision, because he or she was a part of it. The irony of this example is that it eventually forces all the decisions on the back-shooter, as other people become aware of the game and refuse to play. As a result, this person frequently feels overwhelmed by all the work.

Bullying

This is one of the oldest tricks in the book. The bully is usually somebody who is insecure in the first place. This doesn't help deal with his behavior, but it helps to understand that he or she is compensating for perceived weaknesses. I used to think that the way to handle this person was by being just as tough as he or she is. Until one day, I heard an audiotape that suggested a better approach in dealing with bullies.[2] Let them blow off steam, get it out of their systems, then ask what you can do to help. Try it, it works better.

Gatekeeping

One way to control relationships is by gatekeeping, or channeling. Gatekeeping is a normal part of the working of the chain of command, where information is passed up and down the chain, and issues are handled at the appropriate level. This is a way to control information and action. This is maladaptive when someone injects himself or herself between the normal participants in a relationship. It interferes with the organization by taking power from those who are supposed to use it, and placing it in other hands. The ultimate effect is that the structure of the organization is undermined. You can spot gatekeeping when someone avoids notifying you of changes which affect your job, acts as an intermediary between you and your supervisors and associates, or provides indirect feedback on situations in which you are directly involved.

You may not be able to eliminate gatekeeping behavior, but you can control it by being aware of its use and substituting first-hand conversation and your own best judgment for hearsay and innuendo.

The Back Burner

Just because something is important to you doesn't mean it is important to somebody else. Many actions require the coordinated efforts of several people. If one person puts it "on the back burner," they can hold up the whole process. This constitutes mounting behavior. By controlling the situation they put themselves in a position of dominance. One solution to this is your regular tickle file. After a certain amount of follow-up, the person who is dragging his or her feet will get going. But remember, you catch more bees with honey than with vinegar. Gentle persistence is the watchword. Save confrontation for the times when it is absolutely necessary.

Stabbing in the back, sniping, back-shooting, bullying, gatekeeping, and the back burner are examples of mounting behavior. In each case, one person expressed dominance over another by controlling the situation, which enabled them to "get on somebody's back," figuratively mounting them. Grooming behavior is just the opposite. By grooming somebody, you are extending friendship, warmth and cooperation.

GROOMING BEHAVIOR

Back in our imaginary zoo, we also see animals stroking each others' fur, occasionally picking out a piece of dirt or a flea. The one who is being groomed seems to enjoy it. It is unlikely that your boss or associate will pick a flea off you or do anything so overt as to openly massage you, but grooming behavior is an essential part of any relationship. Here are some examples.

The Compliment

A sincere compliment is a joy to us all. In the day-to-day world of making things happen, it is an easy thing to forget to do. Good managers remember and give praise freely. You can too. But the praise must be sincere. It takes a continuous flow of stroking or grooming to create an atmosphere that will tolerate the many stresses of daily work. An example that is frequently used is that of the "atta boys" and the "aw shucks." The game is played as follows: When somebody does something good, you give them an "atta boy" award. When they goof up, you give them an "aw shucks." There is only one problem. One "aw shucks" wipes out all "atta boys." People are like that. One negative comment can wipe out a lot of goodwill. It takes a steady flow of grooming to build a solid relationship.

Consideration

We don't always agree with one another but it is particularly frustrating when you don't think the other person is listening to your point of view. Therefore, it is important to give full consideration to the other person's thoughts and feelings before taking action. It takes more discipline and time to take this approach, but you will probably find something of merit in the other person's ideas. If you are listening to others, you improve your decisions as well as your working relationship.

Facilitation

In practice, to facilitate (to help or assist) means stepping aside, concentrating your efforts on getting the ideas and actions of other people applied to a particular challenge. You aid, you assist, you encourage, you cheerlead, you stroke, you compliment, you may even help focus, and you may referee, but you don't take control. This is an extremely useful technique, and it's fun. Among the most famous facilitators are the matchmakers common to many cultures, who unofficially bring potential mates together. The benefits of this example can be argued, but the issue is more one of conformance to requirements rather than the effectiveness of the process. Provided that facilitation does not extend to manipulation, it can be a useful tool.

Integrity

We talked about integrity earlier on. When you have integrity, you put yourself in the position to be honest on issues, and respectfully agree, disagree, or sidestep an issue without creating confusion on the part of your associates. Without integrity, people will spend an amazing amount of time trying to figure out what you are REALLY trying to do.[3]

MANIPULATION

Manipulation is the third type of individual behavior commonly seen in organizations. Manipulation occurs when we trick people into doing something. The manipulator is doing something that is in his or her best interest, while pretending to help the other person. People eventually see this for exactly what it is, and it is a major turnoff. Here are a few of the most common forms of manipulation.

The Alligator

There is a part of our brain called the amygdala. It is responsible for a reaction called the "rage reaction." It is an ancient part of the brain from an evolutionary point of view, and its actions remind me of the alligator. In our imaginary tour through the zoo, we can observe the alligator lying nearly motionless until food is in sight. All of a sudden, it strikes then quickly returns to nearly absolute stillness. The rage reaction works like that. Have you ever heard the statement, "He really saw red"? The rage reaction may be what the bull feels when it charges. Every now and then, someone who is typically easygoing and even-tempered "sees red." Then, watch out. Eventually this will pass, and the person will probably feel some remorse although he or she may be too embarrassed to apologize. It is important to distinguish between this instant, off-guard, rage response and other forms of anger. It usually means that you have hit a sensitive spot, or as some people call it "hot button." Now you have some good information you can use constructively. This person has told you something about himself or herself. If you are listening, you can work with it. Later, when the person is in a more relaxed mood, you can take your time and discuss in a nonthreatening way what it was that made them mad.

To the extent that this is behavior that occurs once in a while, it may be a true expression of fear or anger. To the extent that it is a deliberate display, it is manipulative. If it occurs frequently, or if the rage is extreme, we're not dealing with a quality improvement problem and we should not offer a quality improvement solution. Having worked on psychiatric wards as well as in business offices, I have to confess that I have frequently observed similar behaviors in both places. Suffice it to say that when someone is not in control of his or her emotions, you are better off picking another time to discuss your improvement suggestions.

Assumption

Basing actions on assumption is widely known to be ineffective and frequently leads to wasted time and effort. Assumption is frequently a convenient way for people to avoid the direct action they know is required. They conveniently assume that you were going to do it. Dirty trick, right? To the extent that the act is deliberate (and some of my best-organized friends have been known to make convenient assumptions), it is manipulative behavior.

Hidden Agenda

An agenda is simply a list of the actions you have planned. A hidden agenda is what you really want, but don't tell anybody. For example, taking your mechanic friend out for a "ride," when you really want him to check your transmission. Unless you are an outstanding manipulator (some people are), the hidden agenda will eventually be discovered and you will be discredited. You can spot someone who is using a hidden agenda because their actions don't seem to make common sense. Once you discover the real agenda, everything falls into place.

Lip Service

Lip service occurs when somebody supports your idea on the surface, complimenting it in public, but quietly refuses to take any action that will support the idea. It is among the most frustrating things that somebody can do. When you think about it from a common sense point of view, it is a stupendous waste of time to support with words what you have no intention of carrying out in actions. So why do it?

SUMMARY

Table 9.1 shows the types of behavior we have discussed here to provide an overall picture of some positive and negative behaviors. You may have observed other variations on behaviors that reflect the same theme. Understanding these behaviors as forms of communication gives you the opportunity to better understand others. If you can spot them in yourself and in others, then you will have a good head start on working in groups to accomplish group quality goals.

MOUNTING	GROOMING	MANIPULATIVE
Back Stabbing	Compliment	Alligator
Sniping	Stroking	Assumption
Bullying	Consideration	Hidden Agenda
Gatekeeping	Facilitation	Lip Service
Back Burner	Integrity	

TABLE 9.1 Types of social behavior

References

1. Koontz, Katy. "Six Ways to Motivate Your Staff." *Sourcebook Magazine* (Summer 1990): 22–28.

2. Bramson, Robert. *Coping with Difficult People.* New York: Dell Publishing Group, 1981 (audiotape).

3. Starker, Steven. *Parathink: The Paranoia of Everyday Life.* Far Hills, NJ: New Horizon Press, 1986, 1.

Suggested Reading

Alessandra, Tony, and Jim Cathcart. *Relationship Strategies.* Chicago: Nightingale-Conant, 1984. (audiotape)

Nirenberg, Jesse S. *Getting Through to People.* Englewood Cliffs, NJ: Prentice-Hall, 1989.

Ten

WORKING WITHIN THE GROUP SETTING

We have been through the five-stage process of personal change which is the beginning of all change. We have itemized and discussed key problem-solving tools, which are useful in producing personal change, as well as the seven-step problem-solving process. We have also considered some of the behaviors you may expect to encounter when you start working to produce change within a group.

Now, it's time to apply the same tools we discussed for creating personal change, but this time in the group situation. There are, of course, some similarities and differences, but the process is the same. At each step, you will adapt the tools already developed in the personal section so the thoughts and feelings of your associates can be taken into consideration. You move from step to step only when you have achieved a consensus within your group. When you listen to those in your group, keep track of their ideas, and show concern, you will not only have a better result, but it will be a more lasting result.

To start out with, we'll go back to our basic flowchart. Before we do this, there is one important point: The surest way to turn somebody off is to exclude them from your group. How you define *we, you, us,* and *them* is very important to your success. An open program is best. If somebody wants to know and expresses interest or curiosity, tell them—no secrets or surprises.

In selecting the group you will work with, you need to include all the skills necessary to accomplish the task at hand; you also need the level of authority necessary to take action. Without these two requirements, you cannot accomplish your objective through the group. Once you have committed to group change, there are five techniques that will be useful:

1. Leadership
2. Brainstorming
3. Voting
4. Team building
5. Facilitation

All of these techniques can be applied throughout the seven-step process. With the possible exception of the data collection phase, all techniques can be applied at all stages as needed.

Keep in mind that the larger a project is, the longer it will take. Be patient.

LEADERSHIP

It is impossible for an organization to undergo significant change without the support of its leader. It is impossible for most leaders to accomplish change without the support of their key people. So where does the process start?

It can start anywhere. If that were not true, there would be no need for this book. It can start with you, but it may wind up with the president of your company. As leadership applies to change, it must reside with you until somebody else takes it on.[1]

Most people want to be directed at least part of the time. The leader provides the vision around which the other members of the organization direct their thoughts. If the leader has no vision, then there will be no overriding sense of direction, and change will not occur. So a very important part of being a leader is to provide the vision of success. As you emerge from your own world into the group setting, it is a good time to check your vision and consider how you can best communicate it to others.

There is also a need for structure within the organization. The structure will determine the way in which change will be implemented. For instance, in a small, loose organization with a few key people, you may get the opportunity to promote your idea personally. On the other hand, in a large, highly structured organization, a pilot group might be selected or a committee or department assigned to review your idea.

The many courses offered in leadership are evidence of the desire to see improvement in this area. As a member of an organization, you need the support of your supervisor if you want to implement change. A good dose of salesmanship training helps you sell your ideas to your supervisor. Once the pitch has been made, his or her response will tell you where you stand. Remember, if you are committed to change (which you should definitely be if you want others to participate), you are the leader until somebody else takes on the project.

Sales training programs point out that the average industrial sale is made on the fifth to the seventh sales call. If that is true, you shouldn't be discouraged if your boss tells you "no" for the first time. Instead of being discouraged, try to identify his or her objections and plan to overcome them on the next attempt.[2] This, too, can be viewed as a process. Go through your seven steps. Bosses can have good ideas, too. Maybe the objections will provide you with additional improvement opportunities.

BRAINSTORMING

Brainstorming with a group is similar to individual brainstorming, but a lot more fun. There are a few simple rules to follow, and any group can brainstorm.

- No negative comments by anybody about anything.
- Do not try to qualify or analyze ideas.
- Extra credit for building on somebody else's idea.
- The leader asks questions, clarifies, and writes notes.

An easel pad is very helpful in this process. Use bold writing and tape each page up on the wall, if possible, as you finish. You may wind up with a whole wall full of ideas and each one may feed many others.

Remember, the idea of brainstorming is to get as many ideas out as possible. If you make negative statements, people will clam up. If you stop to analyze an idea, you may lose momentum and sacrifice other valuable ideas.

Here's another idea. It's a cheap trick, but it works. Bring a bag of goodies such as hard candy, trinkets, handouts. Use them liberally. At first, give one out each time someone comes up with an idea. Once the ideas start flowing, back off and give them out with the ideas that get some response from the others in the group. After a few minutes, you won't be able to write fast enough to keep up with all the good ideas.

VOTING

In goal selection with a group, it may be necessary to vote on issues to achieve a consensus. Why? Because you eventually need everybody's support. If you don't go through this step, someone may block your program, probably at a most unfortunate time. Let's take a moment to define consensus: general agreement, but not always perfect harmony.

In achieving consensus, we are not trying to get 100 percent agreement on everything. The objective of the process is to identify those actions which all members agree to do (or in other words, they will not resist). Use a numerical voting standard and one vote per person, and you can't go too far wrong.

Remember that a group project has the same needs as an individual one:

- It must be doable within a reasonable time frame.
- It must have a measurable objective.

Both of these items are necessary to provide for a sense of accomplishment.

TEAM BUILDING

Team building can be a long, drawn-out process. One reason is that there are so many opportunities to turn people off. Another reason is that there are many excuses for not taking action. As a result, it can take great discipline to build a team. Here are a few ideas which will pay you back tenfold:

- Praise in public, criticize in private.
- Provide for even participation of all team members.
- Keep the group varied; don't load it up with people who all think the same way.

The bottom line is that all players must want to be on the team. If they don't, then they will be in your way. If you have chosen your team well, this will not be a problem.

In order to be an effective team, members must go through the phases of change together, that is, denial that there is a problem, anger over the existence of the problem, negotiation of the issue, depression (or a decision on a solution), and acceptance (or an action on the decision).

One final note: not everybody is cut out to be a team player. For some people, it is just not their style although they may have many helpful ideas and they may have skills or authority you need on your team. Work with them on a one-on-one basis, and keep them informed, and you will still have a valuable ally, even though they are not officially on your team.

In working with a team, it is critically important to work hard on step one of the process, developing a rock-solid objective statement. The team must agree on where it is headed, if all team members are all to wind up at the same end. Your clear vision regarding the reason for the team will help get things off to a good start.

THE VALUE OF A FACILITATOR

What is a facilitator? A facilitator is a person who teaches, provides background information, and helps the process along. There are two types, each with its own benefits.

An inside facilitator is someone from within your organization who is trained in quality improvement concepts and group dynamics. Training and using an inside facilitator provides more skills in-house, and is an excellent way to find future leaders.

An outside facilitator is typically an "expert." The main advantage of the outside person is they can provide educated guidance, unbiased by the internal politics of the organization.

The facilitator is the one who keeps the group process intact. The value of the concept of facilitation lies in the attitude of supporting and encouraging others to work together. This can be a useful attitude to have.

SUMMARY

The five-stage process of change is not different just because more than one person is involved. Nor does the seven-step improvement process change. The techniques of leadership, brainstorming, voting, team building, and facilitation can be applied to shepherd your group through the process with a minimum of pain. By being aware of the stages of denial, anger, negotiation, depression, and acceptance, you can frequently see where individuals and teams are in the process of change, and overcome obstacles which may fall in your way. By understanding where your team is in the problem-solving process, you can select the tools that will facilitate your progress.

References

1. Jongaeward, Dorothy, ed. *Everybody Wins*. Reading, MA: Addison-Wesley, 1973.

2. Ziglar, Zig. *Selling Your Way to the Top*. Chicago, IL: Nightingale-Conant, (audiotape), 1990.

Suggested Reading

Dedication and Desire: Red Auerbach's System for Success. Waterford, CT: Bureau of Business Practice, 1985 (videotape).

Lombardi: Commitment to Excellence. Waterford, CT: Bureau of Business Practice, 1973 (videotape).

Peters, Tom, Robert Townsend. *Excellence in the Organization*. Chicago: Nightingale-Conant, 1990 (audiotape).

Section Four

CHANGING MANAGEMENT ATTITUDES

Eleven

CHANGING MANAGEMENT ATTITUDES

Changing management attitudes: Why would you want to do a thing like that? Maybe their attitudes are just fine. If your company has an established quality improvement program, if it is superbly organized and managed, if it is making money hand over fist, and if there are no imaginable threats to its corporate well-being on the horizon, if its employees are healthy and happy, highly compensated, and work in an environment of enlightened mutual respect, if there are never any problems and every aspect of your business works perfectly, then you don't need to change your management attitudes . . . *yet.*

Even if the above situation exists, how much would you bet on its continued existence? As we said before, life is change and we can count on regular doses of change in our personal and professional lives.

In order to deal with the issue of changing management, we need a framework for consideration of what management is, who the manager is, what is the relative need for change, and what is the level of interest in changing a particular item. Once these factors have been identified, we can develop a plan to accomplish our objectives. We will examine each of the four areas, one at a time, to paint the entire picture. Since accomplishing change outside of yourself involves others, it is important to understand relationships and how they work. You will need to become skilled in dealing with both the thoughts and the feelings of your associates. By understanding the types of people and relationships you are dealing with, while at the same time being aware of where you are in the process of change, you will have a useful frame of reference with which to accomplish your objectives.

WHO AM I?

What you accomplish depends, in part, on how you view yourself and how you are viewed by others. We will be building a different kind of organization chart based on relationships, and with you at the center. By understanding who you are, and your position in the organization, you can learn which type of relationship you need to develop and which tools to use. Alessandra and Cathcart suggest that there are four basic behavior styles.[1] I use their analysis as examples here. Although this is not the only method to view personalities, I have found this one to be very useful. Since effective communication is based on self-respect, understanding yourself is the first step to good communications. Consider the behavior styles shown in Figure 7.2 and give some thought to which pattern best suits you. If you really want to get your eyes opened, ask some people you are comfortable with which type they think suits you. You may be surprised by the answer.

Using behavior style as a starting point, let's consider the types of relationships you deal with: subordinates, peers, and bosses. With subordinates, *you* are management, and consequently it may be your own attitude that needs to change.

WHO ARE THEY?

As shown in Figure 11.1, you are constantly involved in a variety of relationships and each must be handled differently. In the case of your subordinates, you are the boss so they are looking to you for leadership and management. With your peers, you are frequently negotiating to gain support for your idea because you are probably competing for certain resources. Finally, with your supervisors or bosses, you are selling your idea to liberate assets to accomplish your goal.

Figure 11.1 shows the lenses or filters through which people look at each other. This concept applies equally no matter what level in the organization you are dealing with. Everybody has lenses through which they look. These invisible lenses focus statements made by others into a view held by the listener. We all filter information we receive, deliberately or not. Since each of us has

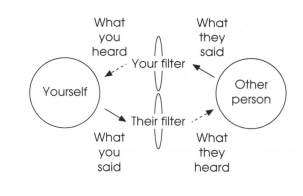

FIGURE 11.1 Filtering information

a different point of view, the same set of information may look different to different people. The need then is to break through the natural barriers which exist and find the common ground. As you work at higher and higher levels in your organization, the time it takes to get results increases. Some things that help build and tear down barriers are shown in Figure 11.2. When you and another person share a common vision there is no barrier. Some activities lower barriers among individuals, while others raise barriers.

With each group (bosses, peers, and subordinates) you will be applying your seven-step process to the relationship, and using communication skills to accomplish your objectives. You will be on the lookout for particular types of behaviors, and be prepared to deal effectively with them. You will also consider these behaviors in yourself and make sure that you are using the positive ones. The *Excellence in the Organization* tape series by Peters and Townsend gives some great examples of positive organizational behavior.[2]

EVALUATING THE ORGANIZATION

In order to get a general idea of the scope of change possible in your group or organization, it helps to get a "snapshot" of where your managers' thinking is at this point in time. One of the best

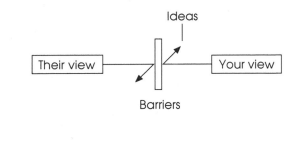

FIGURE 11.2 Overcoming barriers

LOWERING BARRIERS	RAISING BARRIERS
Common world view	Different world view
Same information	Different information
Similar personality	Different personality
High self-esteem	Low self-esteem
Same constraints	Different constraints
General situation helps	General situation hurts

I've seen is Crosby's management maturity grid, shown in Figure 11.3,[3] which you can use to evaluate your organization. For now, however, let's continue with the basic ideas we developed in the first few chapters, and see if they apply to organizations as well as individuals. If you believe that you can influence your organization, it will probably be in ever-widening waves, like dropping a pebble into a smooth lake. Taking this example, you will be mostly concerned with those managers you work with on a regular basis. Ask these questions about yourself, your boss, and your organization:

- Is there an awareness of the need for change?
- Have needs been prioritized?
- Is there a vision of the expected result?
- Have concrete indicators been established?
- Are the indicators being monitored?

We never know exactly what's on someone else's mind, but we can look for evidence based on words and actions. Since words without actions amount to lip service, what we're really looking for are actions. Remember the phrase "what gets measured, gets done." By evaluating where you, your supervisors, and your associates are in this process, you can identify where you should begin in the process of change. What you are doing here is applying your process to their process. In order to achieve your goal, you must know where they are and what process they are applying, if any.

As always, we must advance stepwise because we know that if we skip a step, we will eventually need to return to it and do it right. When this happens, we may have to undo and then redo all the work after that step.

A typical situation involves Lucy, who works for a community theater. Lucy handles the telephone, answering inquiries and documenting reservations as they are called in. She recognizes that there is no one to take over for her when she is away from the telephone for other work, for lunch, or for days off. She has discussed the matter with her boss and her coworkers, but no action has been taken yet.

Table 11.1 shows things from Lucy's perspective. As you can see, she indicates the position of each group. Since this is a small group, Lucy has only three categories; herself, her boss, and others. In a larger organization, a manager may consider her fellow managers as a separate group.

By analyzing the situation, Lucy can see that although her fellow employees are aware of a need, they do not see it as a priority matter. The boss doesn't see that there is a problem. Maybe there isn't. After collecting some facts, like amount of time away from the phone, average number of reservations booked in a day, and maybe even some concrete examples of lost business, Lucy can have a good basis for further discussions with the boss and others.

By understanding the stage of the process that each individual or group is in, she can methodically work through the process with them. The facts themselves will determine whether there is a need for work with the whole group or with individuals.

In this example, her boss is happy and will continue to be in that state until Lucy and her peers start beating down the door with

QUALITY MANAGEMENT MATURITY GRID

Rater _____   Unit _____

Measurement Categories	State I: Uncertainty	Stage II: Awakening	Stage III: Enlightenment	Stage IV: Wisdom	Stage V: Certainty
Management understanding and attitude	No comprehension of quality as a management tool. Tend to blame quality department for "quality problems."	Recognizing that quality management may be of value but not willing to provide money or time to make it all happen.	While going through quality improvement program learn more about quality management; becoming supportive and helpful.	Participating. Understand absolutes of quality management. Recognize their personal role in continuing emphasis.	Consider quality management an essential part of company system.
Quality organization status	Quality is hidden in manufacturing or engineering departments. Inspection probably not part of organization. Emphasis on appraisal and sorting.	A stronger quality leader is appointed but main emphasis is still on appraisal and moving the product. Still part of manufacturing or other.	Quality department reports to top management, all appraisal is incorporated and manager has role in management of company.	Quality manager is an officer of company; effective status reporting and preventive action. Involved with consumer affairs and special assignments.	Quality manager on board of directors. Prevention is main concern. Quality is a thought leader.
Problem handling	Problems are fought as they occur; no resolution; inadequate definition; lots of yelling and accusations.	Teams are set up to attack major problems. Long-range solutions are not solicited.	Corrective action communication established. Problems are faced openly and resolved in an orderly way.	Problems are identified early in their development. All functions are open to suggestion and improvement.	Except in the most unusual cases, problems are prevented.
Cost of quality as % of sales	Reported: unknown Actual: 20%	Reported: 3% Actual: 18%	Reported: 8% Actual: 12%	Reported: 6.5% Actual: 8%	Reported: 2.5% Actual: 2.5%
Quality improvement actions	No organized activities. No understanding of such activities.	Trying obvious "motivational" short-range efforts.	Implementation of the 14-step program with thorough understanding and establishment of each step.	Continuing the 14-step program and starting Make Certain.	Quality improvement is a normal and continued activity.
Summation of company quality posture	"We don't know why we have problems with quality."	"Is it absolutely necessary to always have problems with quality?"	"Through management commitment and quality improvement we are identifying and resolving our problems."	"Defect prevention is a routine part of our operation."	"We know why we do not have problems with quality."

XXPMUSOOOBO

FIGURE 11.3 Crosby's management maturity grid

INDICATOR QUESTION	BOSS	SELF	PEERS
Is there an awareness of the need for change?	No	Yes	Yes
Have the needs been prioritized?	No	Yes	No
Is there a vision of the expected result?	No	Yes	Yes
Have concrete indicators been established?	No	Yes	No
Are the indicators being monitored?	No	No	No

TABLE 11.1 Organizational review

complaints or suggestions for improvement. She will be working with her boss on awareness of the need for change.

Her peers are in various states. One likely condition is that they all want change, but their priorities are different. That being the case, Lucy will be looking for common ground to facilitate changes that will be beneficial to, and therefore supported by, her peers.

After collecting the necessary facts, Lucy has prioritized the areas in which she will work. Her thinking goes like this:

1. I will first discuss the information I have gathered with my peers and my boss to get us into the same "world."

2. During discussions, I will be alert for indications of their acceptance of these ideas and look for specific objections.

3. If I encounter specific objections, I will not try to argue. I will identify solutions which will overcome the objections and schedule a later meeting.

4. I will continue to work with both boss and peers until I achieve a consensus.

MANAGING THE MANAGER

Let's start with a general statement: *Managers are people, too.* Each person has his or her own set of hopes, desires, fears, constraints, and experiences that combine together to produce each person's "reality." You need not go too much farther than this to proceed with any issue. In other words, just listen carefully to each person. As you discuss your issues with them, you can identify their reality and find points in common with your reality.[4] Remember that we are working both on a thinking level and a feeling level. This common ground provides a solid base from which to move forward. The amount of common ground at the start determines how much more you may have to build, or how long the project may take. You may even find there is no common ground with which to start. Now you have something to work on.

BEHAVIOR STYLES

We all think with different parts of our brain.[5] Because different areas of our brain are designed to do different things, our behavior differs based on which part of the brain is more active. Figure 7.2 shows the common behavior styles.

Table 11.2, coupled with our model of change, can give us some clues which help us find the common ground with our bosses more effectively to accomplish changes which are important to us. The table shows how to relate your seven-step process to each of the four basic types.

If your boss won't let you get close enough to get a glimpse of his or her personal style, then you must work on the relationship immediately. Without knowing what he or she wants, you don't stand a chance of meeting their requirements. As a result, you are not able to develop credibility with your boss and your ability to influence change upward is minimized.

In addition to this grid perspective, there are several other concepts that are useful in making sense out of the boss' behavior.

The danger is that we could unduly pigeonhole our leader. As long as we keep listening to what others actually say and do, such dangers are minimized and the advantages are multiplied because we will always be getting feedback on each action.

The Basic Operating Fantasy

We all have a certain fantasy image of ourselves, sometimes referred to as our heart of hearts or our alter ego. Even though our

	MANAGEMENT TYPE			
STEP IN PROGRESS	Thinker	Director	Socializer	Relater
Problem ID	Show logic	Show vision	Show path to results	Show role of people
Problem Analysis	Deliberate, methodical development	Don't dwell on method	Convince of ability to get results	Convince of ability to work with people
Planning	Assure that plan is internally consistent	If he has bought the idea, the planning will be up to you.	"Don't bother me with the plan, just do it."	"Keep me involved, so I can feel included."
Data collecting	Make sure you are consistent	Not concerned with nuts and bolts	Pressure to produce results	Concerned more with people than results.
Data interpretation	Probably wants to review data	Notify of success, fit vision	Present data in terms of results	"Let me know how you are doing."
Action	Guide me through your logic	How does the action fit for vision?	Relate the action to results	How does the action fit the people?
Appraisal	Tie it all back together with logic	How do the results affect the vision?	Did I get the results I wanted —tangible?	Everybody happy?

TABLE 11.2 Management Type Interaction Grid

managers may not communicate this directly to us, they may give us clues to help us to understand what they are all about. Although this idea can apply equally to anybody, if we wish to succeed, it is vitally important that we understand our manager's basic operating fantasy and attach our program to it. Listen creatively and you can find the answers. Depending on the personality types of you and the manager, you may have an advantage or disadvantage. It will be much easier to support your boss's view if you can relate your objectives to it, rather than to try to sell him or her on some other world view.

Dealing with Fears

When working with others, keep an eye out for the "alligator" mentioned earlier. Our lesser day-to-day irritations or fears can be expressed directly, but the major ones are frequently kept concealed. When you are discussing an idea with your manager, keep an eye out for this one. It will frequently mean that you have touched one of these fears. Now you must consider how you can proceed without raising this sensitivity again.[6,7]

Approach-Avoidance

Another useful way of looking at situations is the approach-avoidance process. This has been a basic in the field of psychology for many years.[8] In essence, the concept states that decisions can be typified by the types of alternatives that must be considered, for instance, an approach-approach problem is one in which there are two positive options to consider.

An approach-avoidance situation is easier, because you wish to approach one alternative while avoiding another. Obviously, you select the option you wish to approach. Many management decisions are complicated, having multiple options that we wish to either approach or avoid. You will want to increase the value in the mind of your manager of the approach factors associated with your project, and also increase the value of the avoidance factors in *not* proceeding with your project. Getting a positive decision depends on your effectiveness in drawing attention to these values. Figure 11.4 shows a graphic view of the approach-avoidance conflict. This person's "scale" is heavier with avoidance factors, so he or she will move away from those factors. If you know which factors are important, you can tip the scale.

Making the Dog Crazy

I once read a fascinating article about how a psychologist induced symptoms of mental illness in a dog by making it impossible for the dog to make a decision.[9] Here's how it worked: The dog was put in a cage with two pedals, each one with a picture over it. One

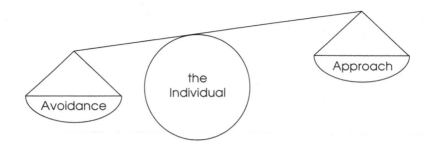

FIGURE 11.4 The approach-avoidance conflict

was a picture of a circle, while the other was an oval. In order to get food, the dog had to step on the pedal with the circle.

Once trained, the dog could regularly press the correct pedal to receive its food. Then the game was changed. The pictures were gradually modified, with the circle looking more oval-like, and the oval looking more circle-like. As the distinction became less clear, the dog began to howl and carry on. Why? It could not distinguish between alternatives. This could be used as an example of how to increase stress. You can prevent or delay a decision, and probably introduce stress into a relationship if you ask for a decision without providing clear alternatives. Although not deliberate in many cases, we frequently confuse others by presenting unclear alternatives. If you find that a decision is driving you crazy, consider clarifying the alternatives by using the seven-step process.

Here's an example involving Xavier, who works in the warehouse. He is frequently asked to assist in the tool room as well. Many times, Xavier is already falling behind in his first job, while he is being asked at the same time to do other work. His first reaction is stress. Xavier thinks the matter through, and finds that his boss may simply not be aware of his situation. Next time the boss asks him to cover for the tool room when he is already behind in the warehouse, he explains to his boss what needs to be done in the warehouse and why. He then asks his boss which the boss would rather have done first. He may not like the answer, but at least the objective will be clear.

Fear of Failure/Fear of Success

As we mentioned earlier, many management decisions are multiple approach-avoidance decisions. On the avoidance side, there may be a dilemma: If we succeed we might change in such a way that nobody will like us, while if we fail, we will be embarrassed. Putting this into our approach-avoidance example, we can see that the clear solution is to increase the value of the approach factors, making them as real or tangible as possible, and presenting them in a format which will take best advantage of the behavior style of the manager in question. If we do not do this, we run the risk of catching him or her on the horns of the dilemma between fear of success and fear of failure.

Take Tom, for example, who has wanted to streamline the billing system for some time now. But he can't seem to get the cooperation of his supervisor, Ms. Williams. By collecting his facts, particularly on how much time is wasted and how many errors are made on the billings, the cost of additional calls from the credit department, and the aggravation of the customers, Tom builds the approach factor for solutions. By discussing this issue with others in the organization, Tom has begun to build a constituency for this issue. Others also begin to ask Ms. Williams if something can be done to streamline billing.

Resistance to Change

Resistance to change is normal.[10] Expect to encounter it in yourself and others. Your greatest allies are patience and determination; your greatest enemies are fear and discouragement. Rarely is an idea sold on the first try; it can take many more attempts, depending on how complicated the issue is. Expect to work hard. Your objectives will eventually be met if on each try you make sure you ask the right questions, understand the objections, and work to specifically overcome the objections.

PUTTING IT ALL TOGETHER

Now, it's time to put the whole picture together. First, because we are aware that each of us has a separate reality, we have structured our listening in order to better understand the realities of our associates. Second, we have selected early projects which are doable, to create a positive track record. Third, by listening carefully to our managers (and other associates), we have identified their position in the seven-step process of change. If they are in steps two through seven, we can engage the process at that step, and work together with them to achieve the best result. If they are in step one (they frequently will be, because you have not yet convinced them that anything needs to be changed), then we must answer the following questions:

- Is there an awareness of the need for change?
- Have needs been prioritized?
- Is there a vision of the expected result?
- Have concrete indicators been established?
- Are the indicators being monitored?

If they are not aware of a need for change, you must take them through the five steps of denial, anger, negotiation, depression (or decision), and acceptance (or action) before you can produce lasting change.

Your manager will certainly have priorities. Your job is to discover them so you can put your recommendations in a context meaningful to him or her. Having accomplished that, you will know if you need to change their priorities, or simply get them to act more constructively on their own priorities.

Rule One

Unless your manager or other associate engages you in an activity at a later level, you must assume you are at step one.

Rule Two

If someone engages you at a later step, first review each step with them, starting at step one, to assure that you have a common vision, and the steps were executed correctly.

Redefinition and Coalition

Any time you approach another person with a suggestion for change, you initiate a process. The first step in this process is the merging of your world view with their world view. When your information and their information are combined, you may both change your opinions about the situation.

Imagine a typical situation: You are aware of a change in a close relationship. Anguishing over how to broach the subject with your close friend, you finally find the right opportunity to mention the problem. Much to your surprise, you find that the friend has sensed the same problem. After sharing information, you find that the source of the change was insignificant and that there is really no problem with the relationship at all.

This example is very generic because it represents a common occurrence, even for those who consider themselves good or even excellent communicators. The fact is that the encounter must occur with the right timing, and the information must be shared for the process of change to occur.

The stage for change has now been set. You are both working from the same set of information and your views have merged, at least to the point that they can be discussed. There are now several possible directions for forward movement. Figure 11.5 shows some possible outcomes, using the diagram we have built up over the previous chapters. Diagramming the process can aid in understanding decisions.

First, the other person is unaware of the need for change. You have chosen the right timing and are successful in your presentation, having applied your best skills and used all available tools in preparing for this encounter. There are several possible outcomes:

a. He or she tells you to do it. You now have the control and the mandate to go forward. Congratulations.

b. Let's do it. He or she wants to be a part of this picture. Responsibility is not clear cut. But you are the situational leader until the other person takes responsibility.

c. I'll do it. He or she takes it out of your hands. You are now in a position to be supportive, but not to take direct action.

d. I'll think about it. You didn't close the sale. Get a firm date for an answer, and have responses ready to counter any objections.

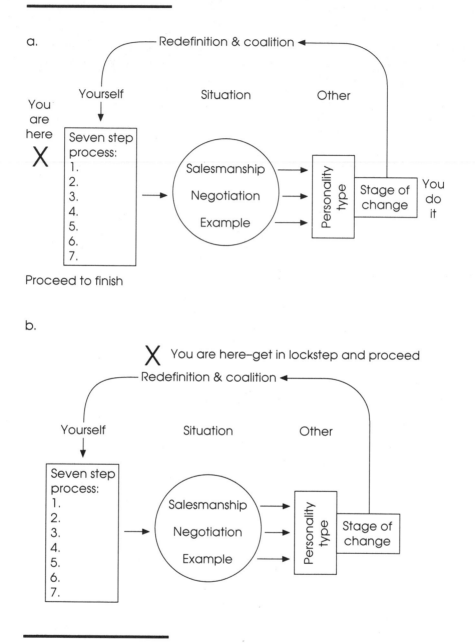

FIGURE 11.5 Presentation decision tree

c.

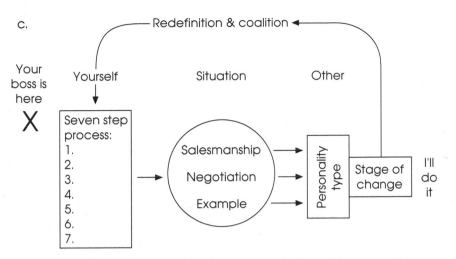

Boss has the ball, find out how to help and be supportive

d.

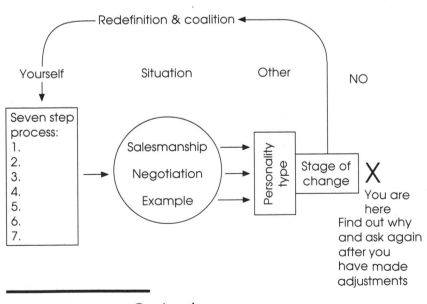

FIGURE 11.5 Continued

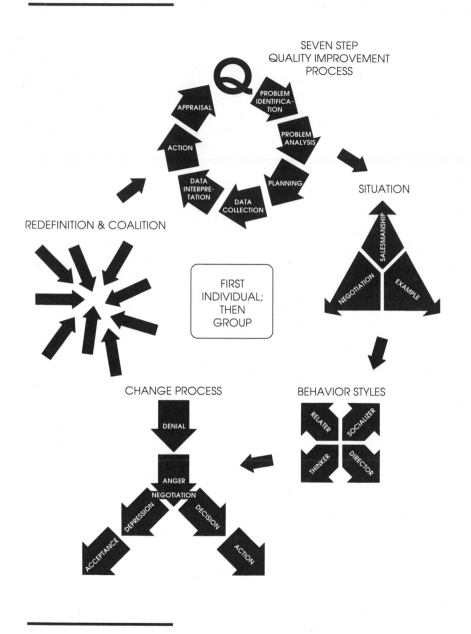

FIGURE 11.6 The whole picture

There are two excellent pieces of advice I have picked up along the way:

1. Never propose anything to another person unless you are prepared to take full responsibility for making it happen. This goes back to your personal integrity. If something is not worth doing, why would you suggest that somebody else do it? You should always be prepared to be put to the test.

2. Control the presentation. When making any kind of a proposal, you must always be alert to distracting influences and avoid them like the plague. If you can control the presentation, you can frequently control the result.

THE IMPORTANCE OF SENIOR MANAGEMENT

If you plan to make a significant change to your organization, you must have the support of senior management. In fact, it must be seen by others as their idea from start to finish. Without this level of support, other managers and employees are likely to think your idea is unimportant. In fact, without this level of support, your process will be unimportant to your organization, regardless of the depth of your feelings on the subject.

From a practical standpoint, this means you must use all your skills to get your ideas to the top. When you commit to change outside yourself, you are undertaking a long and difficult journey. It is not unusual for this journey to take five, ten, or fifteen years in a large organization, even with top management support. Once your president or chairman of the board has taken on this project, it becomes his or her responsibility to get the other staff focused, trained, engaged in regular evaluations, etc. You can then play a supportive role in helping them make progress.

Remember, you are on "square one" until you get off. In terms of senior management that means that you cannot have a company-wide quality program until it comes from the "big boss." It won't come from the boss until he or she is convinced that the process will benefit the company in the long term and not cost too much in the short term. You won't convince him or her until you have a program in mind and a few concrete examples under your belt to show. All this won't happen overnight, but it can be done.

Create your vision, then systematically follow it. There are no guarantees of success. There is only the assurance that if you do nothing, you will accomplish nothing. Personal change, interpersonal skills, understanding of others, the group change process, and redefinition/coalition form a never-ending cycle that can be influenced by you. Where do you want to start?

References

1. Alessandra, Tony, and Jim Cathcart. *Relationship Strategies.* Chicago: Nightingale-Conant, 1990.

2. Peters, Tom, Robert Townsend. *Excellence in the Organization.* Chicago: Nightingale-Conant, 1988. (audiotape)

3. Crosby, Philip. *Quality Is Free.* New York: McGraw-Hill, 1979, 38–39.

4. Suarez, R., Roger C. Mills, and Darlene Stuart. *Sanity, Insanity and Common Sense.* New York: Fawcett-Columbine (Balentine), 1980.

5. Alessandra, Tony, and Jim Cathcart. *Relationship Strategies.* Chicago: Nightingale-Conant, 1990.

6. Tichy, Noel M., and Mary Anne Devanna. *The Transformational Leader.* New York: John Wiley and Sons, 1990.

7. Rozek, Michael. "Fear of Failure." *Your Company* Vol. 1. (Fall 1990): 24–27.

8. Skinner, B. F. *The Science of Human Behavior.* New York: Free Press, 1953, 59–106 and 171–181.

9. Fontine, E., and G. S. Reynolds. *Introduction to Contemporary Psychology.* San Francisco: W. H. Freeman and Co., 1975, 50–60. The experimenter was Dr. Shengor-Krestovnikova, a student of Pavlov.

10. Tichy, Noel M., and Mary Anne Devanna. *The Transformational Leader.* New York: John Wiley and Sons, 1990.

Suggested Reading

Drucker, Peter F. *The New Realities.* New York: Harper and Row, 1989.

Drucker, Peter F. *The Frontiers of Management.* New York: E. P. Dutton, 1986.

Goldratt, E. M. *Theory of Constraints.* Croton-on-Hudson: North River Press, 1990.

Russell, J. P. *The Quality Master Plan.* Milwaukee: ASQC Quality Press, 1990.

Twelve

WHERE TO GO FROM HERE

Recent worldwide political turmoil gives us a serious reason to ask ourselves what things deserve our attention. From moment-to-moment and day-to-day, we have the opportunity to reevaluate our situation and our priorities. Every decision we make may not be the best. We have to get past those errors, and move forward. To dwell on them accomplishes nothing, yet if we can learn a little bit from each transaction, we will be engaged in a process of continuous improvement. By applying this process to our lives we can accomplish many things—not overnight, but by improving each action a little bit at a time, every time. But we must each make a personal decision to do it.

This book is about the ideas and concepts, and the tools and techniques of continuous improvement. It has been my experience that these tools and techniques can be molded into a decision process, enabling us to improve our lives, and maybe even the lives of others with whom we have contact. If the concepts we have presented are useful, then each reader will have at least one suggestion for improvement on them. As an old Oriental proverb goes, "It is the poor student who does not surpass his teacher." I encourage you to read the books and listen to the tapes provided at the end of each chapter, and to mold your personal process into a form that works for you.

There are a few key concepts that I hope you will carry with you. The rest is detail, and can be reviewed as needed:

First, change is always a personal process. This process has the specific stages of denial, anger, negotiation, depression, and acceptance. Each stage must be passed through to progress to the next stage. The process must be completed if permanent change is to occur.

Second, the seven-step quality improvement process can be applied to make it easier to pass through the stages of change, and can help us to organize ourselves to accomplish those changes which are worth the effort.

Third, there is a body of well-established problem-solving tools that can be used in defining needs, analyzing data, proposing and selecting solutions, and implementing change. These tools are amply documented, and ready for your use. You can and should use them—they really work.

Fourth, we can only accomplish according to our span of control. If we want to produce changes outside ourselves, we must work with others. The requirements of group change are the same as for personal change, but the whole group must participate. Some behaviors of people as a part of a group and some of the special techniques for working with others have been presented. I encourage you to follow through with further study of group dynamics and team building if you plan to work with groups on a regular basis.

Finally, the importance of senior management to the process of change in an organization cannot be overstated. It is absolutely critical, particularly when it applies to so broad a concept as quality improvement, which affects all aspects of an organization.

Every day of our lives, we have the opportunity to do something positive. By understanding the process of continuous improvement and applying its tools in an organized way, we can improve our odds of success.

Why not start now?

Appendix

COMPARISON OF STRUCTURED TECHNIQUES

INGLE	JURAN	ROSANDER	FLORIDA POWER AND LIGHT	ALCOA
		Step One		
Selection of a theme	Proof of need	Problem identification	Collect improvement opportunities	Define problems and opportunities
	Screen nominations and est. priorities		Prioritize and select opportunities	Select the problem or opportunity
		Step Two		
Cause-and-effect diagram and situation analysis	Diagnosis Analysis of symptoms	Problem analysis	Analyze root causes	Analyze causes and effects
		Step Three		
Setting the target	Formulation of theories	Planning	* continue *	Generate potential actions
	Development of remedies			
		Step Four		
* continue *	* continue *	Data collection	* continue *	* continue *
		Step Five		
* continue *	Proof of remedies	Data analysis	Select solution	Evaluate and select actions
		Step Six		
* continue *	* continue *	Action	Conduct trial implementation	Test effectiveness of action
			Track effectiveness	
		Step Seven		
Confirm results	Control at new level	Appraisal	Implement solution	Implement solution
			Track effectiveness	Monitor

Seven steps serve to conveniently describe the problem-solving process. Here is a comparison of several current programs used as source material for this book.

Glossary

ACTION Step six of the seven-step process of change.

ALLIGATOR A manipulative behavior.

APPRAISAL Step seven of the seven-step process of change.

ASSUMPTION A manipulative behavior.

BACK BURNER A mounting behavior.

BACK-SHOOTING A mounting behavior.

BODY LANGUAGE The physical motions that communicate our feelings to others, frequently without our awareness. One of the four elements of the communication process.

BRAINSTORMING A structured technique for generating ideas.

CAUSE-AND-EFFECT DIAGRAM A graphic technique based around the diagramming of causes and effects in a fishbone style, used to identify root causes which apply to a certain situation. Major "bones" of the fishbone diagram are frequently the five m's. One of the seven basic problem-solving tools.

CHANGE The action of making something different.

CHECKLIST (OR CHECK SHEET) One of the seven basic problem-solving tools.

COMMITMENT A pledge of performance.

COMPLIMENT A grooming behavior and powerful motivator.

CONSENSUS Something agreed to by most of the group, not necessarily agreed to entirely by all members, but which all will support.

CONSTITUENCY A group of people who will support an idea.

CONTROL CHART Any chart used to control a process, usually thought of as a strictly statistical tool with mean, upper and lower control limits, and occurrences plotted. One of the seven basic problem-solving tools.

CONTROL LIMITS Upper and lower control limits are boundaries used to determine when action should be taken.

COST OF POOR QUALITY The sum of all the costs associated with the production of a product that does not conform to the customer's requirements. Because it is frequently much higher than the cost of quality, it forms the economic justification for the phrase "quality is free."

COST OF QUALITY Usually associated with Crosby, the sum of the costs associated with producing a product which conforms to the customer's requirements. See *cost of poor quality.*

CRITERIA Standards by which a judgment is made. (Usually used in plural; singular is criterion.)

CRITICAL PATH The sequence of events that must follow one another in sequence to accomplish a task. Delay in any item on the critical path will delay the accomplishment of the goal.

DATA COLLECTION Step four of the seven-step process of change.

DATA INTERPRETATION Step five of the seven-step process of change.

DECISION MATRIX A problem-solving tool in which options are evaluated by ranking them against several criteria. The ranks are then summarized and the total score used to aid in decision making.

DETERMINATION Firmness of purpose.

ENERGY LEVEL The amount of enthusiasm communicated to others, frequently used by them to evaluate the importance of your activities.

FACILITATOR A person who aids or facilitates a process.

FINISHED You're never finished. You just keep polishing until they take it away.

FISHBONE DIAGRAM See *cause-and-effect diagram.*

FIVE WHYS The process of asking the question "Why?" five times, each time in response to the previous answer, for the purpose of finding the root cause of a situation.

FLOWCHART A graphic method of displaying the elements and decisions involved in a process.

FOUR M'S Man (people), Method, Machine, Materials, frequently used in problem diagnosis.

FOUR W'S (PLUS H) Who, What, When, Where, and How.

GATEKEEPING A mounting behavior.

GANTT CHART A graphic description of activities and associated time frames, used for process control.

GRAPHS Any type of graphic representation of data used to organize or communicate information. One of the seven basic problem-solving tools.

GROOMING BEHAVIOR The process of stroking or grooming another being, used as an expression of friendship or mutuality.

GROUP A collection of individuals brought together by a common vision, sense of purpose, or objective.

GROUP PROCESS The specific process of forming a group.

GROUPTHINK The situation in which the cohesiveness of a group outweighs the judgment of the individual, resulting in group-defensive behavior rather than good decision making.

HIDDEN AGENDA A manipulative behavior.

HISTOGRAM One of the seven basic problem-solving tools.

INDICATE To point out, signify, denote, show, manifest, mark, disclose, or reveal.

INDICATOR The feature monitored in the process of change to point out status and progress of the process.

INFORMATION Data endowed with relevance and purpose.

INPUTS Things provided at the beginning of the process, to which the process is applied.

INTEGRITY Moral wholeness, completeness.

ISHIKAWA DIAGRAM See *cause-and-effect diagram.*

LEADERSHIP The sum total of behaviors that fill the needs of subordinates, including establishing a vision or sense of direction, communicating the vision to the group, deploying the group to accomplish the objective.

LIP SERVICE A manipulative behavior.

LISTENING One of the four elements of the communication process.

MANIPULATIVE BEHAVIOR The process of manipulating others for one's exclusive self-interest while creating the impression of acting in the other's interest.

METHOD A systematic procedure or technique, a particular way of doing things.

MOTIVATION That which leads to action.

MOUNTING BEHAVIOR The process of physically or figuratively climbing on top of another being to express dominance.

NEGOTIATION The act of meeting with another person in order to accomplish action which is beneficial to both.

OUTPUTS The results of the actions, usually acting as inputs to the next process.

OBJECTIVE STATEMENT A sentence that clearly states the objective of an activity and includes or implies an indicator by which accomplishment can be measured.

PARETO CHART A histogram that is organized in order of occurrences to determine if Pareto's law is in effect or to prioritize by frequency of occurrence. One of the seven basic problem-solving tools.

PARETO'S LAW 80% of the occurrences in a distribution will come from 20% of the elements.

PEER One who is at the same organizational level as another.

PLANNING Step three of the seven-step process of change.

PRIORITIES The rankings of individual actions in order of importance or order; which thing to do first.

PROBLEM ANALYSIS Step two of the seven-step process of change.

PROBLEM IDENTIFICATION Step one of the seven-step process of change.

PROCEDURE An organized way of doing things.

PROCESS A series of acts aimed at a single end.

QUALITY Conformance to requirements.

ROOT CAUSE The ultimate cause, which, if corrected, will result in the elimination of the problem.

QUEUING THEORY See *Theory of Lines*.

SCATTER DIAGRAM One of the seven basic problem-solving tools.

SELF-EVALUATION Realistic, factual evaluation of one's own performance. Appraisal on an individual level.

SNIPING A mounting behavior.

STAB IN THE BACK A mounting behavior.

STATISTIC(S) The science of numerical facts.

SYSTEM A group of components organized to accomplish a common purpose.

TALKING One of the four elements of communications.

TEAM BUILDING The result of behaviors which serve to strengthen and encourage the formation of a team.

THEORY X One of MacGregor's management types in which the manager bases his or her actions on the assumption that employees must be controlled.

THEORY OF LINES The science of managing (or queues) lines to accomplish a desired result.

THEORY Y One of MacGregor's management types, in which the manager bases his or her actions on the assumption that employees will do their work if not interfered with.

VISUALIZATION The process of constructing a mental image.

VITAL FEW Juran's phrase used to describe reduction of potential actions to the few most important ones deserving of action.

VOTING A technique for achieving consensus.

WRITING One of the four elements of the communication process.

Index